Faithful Guides

Faithful Guides

*Coaching Strategies for
Church Leaders*

Thomas R. Hawkins

DISCIPLESHIP RESOURCES

P O BOX 340003 • NASHVILLE, TN 37203-0003
www.discipleshipresources.org

ISBN 0-88177-465-0

Library of Congress Control Number 2004116743

TABLE OF CONTENTS

WHO NEEDS A COACH?

"I saw the announcement in yesterday's bulletin saying that the Sunday school needed teachers," Tonya Reynolds said to Sally O'Connor, the Christian Education Director at Living Hope Church. "I feel that God is calling me to teach. I have grown so much as a Christian through the classes here at Living Hope," she continued. "By serving as a Sunday school teacher I can give back some of what I have received. But I don't know much about teaching."

"That's wonderful news," Sally responded. "If you feel God is calling you to teach, we will do all we can to cooperate with the Holy Spirit. We have several experienced teachers who serve as coaches for our newer volunteers. If God has laid it on your heart to teach, I am sure we can find a coach to walk alongside you as you learn to be a successful teacher."

"A coach?" Tonya asked with a puzzled look on her face. "But I don't want to work with the church's volleyball team. I want to help in the Sunday school."

Sally smiled and said, "Coaches are not just for sports teams. Lots of leaders at Living Hope have coaches who help them grow and achieve their goals. They listen, ask good questions, and support others as they develop their ministries. Our coaches help people become the best leaders they imagine God is calling them to be," Sally explained. She assured Tonya that a good coach could help her discover her own strengths and achieve success as a teacher.

A few miles away—on the growing ex-urban edge of the same city—Terri Morgan picked up her telephone and called her coach. Terri's denomination had sent her to plant a new congregation in this growing community. There was so much to do. It was not always clear where she should start or what her first priority should be. Opportunities for ministry always outnumbered available resources. Terri felt she had more to do than she could possibly accomplish. Now, nearly a year into the new church development, she faced tough choices about the direction her ministry should take.

When her denominational executive told her she would have a coach, Terri was puzzled. Her coach was not going to be her supervisor. Nor would he or she be connected to the project's funding and oversight committee. Who was this person and how could he or she be an asset? She had initially resisted the coaching relationship. It seemed like one more person or group to whom she would have to report and be accountable.

Now Terri looked forward to her weekly coaching sessions. Her coach was a good listener. He asked thoughtful questions that allowed her to clarify her own vision, stay focused on her most important tasks, and maintain a healthy balance between her ministry and family. "Without my coaching relationship," she said, "I would never have gotten so far in planting a new congregation here."

Terri's younger brother, Geoffrey, had followed her to seminary. He was now serving his first congregation in a nearby state. "Seminary never prepared me for this," he told his sister. "I feel overwhelmed. I don't know where to start." Drawing on her own positive experience, Terri suggested that her brother find a coach to help him work through the transition from seminary to full-time ministry.

Geoffrey was unsure how such a relationship could add value to his ministry. "What do these coaches do? Will they give me advice?" Geoffrey asked. "Will they be like some sort of therapist? Will they give me books to read and lecture me on what I ought to do—like my seminary professors? What can a coach really know about this congregation and the people in it?"

Terri laughed. "I once wondered the same thing," she answered. "Almost anyone can benefit from having a coach. A coach is not a consultant or teacher or therapist. Coaches are trained to guide others toward greater competence in ministry," Terri explained. "Good coaches can help you learn from your experience so you are more reflective and self-aware in your practice of ministry. They can help you stay focused on the goals you want to achieve. I sometimes think of my coach as a personal learning consultant."

Geoffrey took his older sister's advice. And, several months later, he realized the difference the weekly coaching appointments were making in his ministry. His coach was an excellent listener and knew how to ask questions that drew forth Geoffrey's best thinking and planning. His coach encouraged him to set specific goals and held him accountable for actions to which he had committed himself. Geoffrey's coach helped him become more aware of his own behavior and take responsibility for himself and his ministry.

At one of his monthly ministerial meetings, Geoffrey shared how working with a coach had eased his transition from seminary to full-time ministry. One of his colleagues, Travis Chalmers, added that he too had worked with a coach. "It changed my life," he said. Travis admitted that he might have left the ministry if he had not stumbled inadvertently into a coaching relationship. His coaching experience caused Travis to re-evaluate his ministry. "It transformed how I understood my task as a spiritual leader," he said.

"I now see coaching other leaders as one of my primary responsibilities as pastor at St. Luke Church," Travis added. "A few months ago, a church member shared that he wanted to begin a new men's ministry. Since then, I have been coaching him as he develops this ministry."

Travis described how he saw coaching as a powerful way for the church to carry out Jesus' great commission to make disciples of Jesus Christ for the transformation of the world. "When I coach other leaders in the congregation," Travis continued, "I am helping them grow as disciples of Jesus Christ who have their own gifts and graces for ministry. Earlier in my own ministry, I believed that effectively doing my pastoral tasks—preaching, teaching, and managing church programs—was the measure of my success as a spiritual leader. Then one day I realized my task was to multiply leadership through developing the potential of other leaders. Coaching has given me both the theory and the tools to develop the spiritual leaders around me."

Travis explained that coaching takes more time than distributing reading material or offering training seminars. But the payoff is long-term, not short-term. Coaching's long-term benefit is the development of other leaders who themselves have the capacity to multiply ministry. Previously his focus had been on increasing the number of followers who were church members. Now he coaches people to become self-confident leaders who themselves coach others into spiritual leadership. "Coaching has helped me multiply leadership rather than hoard it as something only I can do," Travis concluded.

Travis, Geoffrey, Terri, Tonya, and Sally are discovering how coaching can multiply ministry. Coaching is about transformation and change. It is about helping people claim and use the gifts for ministry that God has given them. Coaching will become an increasingly important skill as the church moves away from its old pattern of making members toward the new reality of making disciples. A few classes or workshops may have been enough to make members of those already committed to the church. But making disciples and equipping them for ministry in a missional context demands leaders who can walk alongside others, listen to them, ask powerful questions, and guide them toward their own self-discovery and learning.

This book will first explore the roots of today's emphasis on the coaching relationship as an essential strategy for personal and organizational transformation. It will explore how coaching is not something new but instead is deeply rooted in the Bible and in the church's rich historical practices. We will next distinguish coaching from other helping relationships such as consulting, counseling, and spiritual direction. Having reviewed these fundamentals, we will turn to the components and principles of the coaching relationship. Finally, after looking at what happens in a coaching session, we will describe some specific coaching skills.

Coaching is not a difficult or esoteric skill. It is something almost anyone can learn. Spiritual leaders are called to equip the saints for the work of ministry and to make disciples of Jesus Christ for the transformation of the world. Many Christians have a deep desire to fulfill this mission; but they are unsure where to begin. Or they wonder whether they possess the necessary skills. Understanding and implementing the basic principles of coaching is one strategy for empowering church leaders to equip the saints for ministry. As more church leaders adopt a coaching approach, ministry is multiplied. This resource will help you learn how you can be an effective coach who equips and sends forth disciples of Jesus Christ for the work of ministry.

FROM CHAIRPERSON TO COACH

It was perhaps inevitable. Everyone should have anticipated it. Once church groups became teams, leaders had to become coaches. Teams and coaches go together in the same way that people cannot hear "bacon" without thinking of "eggs." Chairpersons, after all, do not lead teams. The Boston Bruins, the Los Angeles Lakers, and the Chicago Bears do not have chairpersons, conveners, or facilitators. Teams have coaches. When congregations adopted the new language of teams and teamwork, their leadership terminology also underwent a gradual transformation. The image of leader as coach slowly crept into the church's vocabulary. Chairpersons may be appropriate for committees; but teams require coaches.

Coaching Is A Hot Topic

We have now reached the tipping point in this transformation of leaders into coaches. References to coaching are everywhere. Coaches are an especially prominent phenomenon in church planting and redevelopment.

In one of his recent books, *Coaching Change: Breaking Down Resistance, Building Up Hope*, (2000) Tom Bandy does not speak of leading change. He proposes instead that we start coaching change. Robert E. Logan, an early leader in the church planting movement, now coordinates CoachNet (2005). CoachNet provides a wide range of face-to-face and online resources for coaching pastoral leaders, particularly new church developers and church redevelopment specialists.

11

Many denominations now expect church planters to have a coach. These coaches help church planters think through vital decisions and stay focused on critical issues. They provide both emotional support and accountability. The coach usually operates outside the supervisory and funding channels of oversight committees or judicatory staff. Coaching is not about evaluation and assessment. It instead provides church planters or redevelopers with a personal catalyst for growth, a champion, and a thinking partner.

A recent church redevelopment initiative in one northeastern presbytery of The Presbyterian Church (USA) assigned coaches to local church transformation teams (2004). These coaches assisted local churches in visioning, planning, and implementing change. In the Illinois Great Rivers Annual Conference of The United Methodist Church, the Congregational Development Committee hopes to create a culture of coaching. They want church planters and redevelopers to have coaches who will walk alongside them (2004). One of the Alban Institute's best-selling books in 2003 was *Redeveloping the Congregation: A How-To for Lasting Change*. Two of its three authors describe themselves as coaches. Each chapter supplements its material with a coaching perspective.

The popularity of coaching is even more pronounced in the corporate world. A friend recently commented that it was difficult to attend the Chamber of Commerce's monthly meeting without speaking either to executives receiving coaching or to individuals offering coaching as a professional service.

As early as 1950, Myles Mace used the term "coaching" in his book, *The Growth and Development of Executives*. Mace emphasized on-the-job coaching as one way to develop an executive's leadership and managerial skills. Over the past half-century, coaching has expanded into a strategy for boosting the career advancement possibilities of promising employees as well as for improving executive performance.

It was not until the early 1990s that coaching received widespread attention. In 1992, Thomas Leonard founded Coach University. Laura Whitworth and some of her associates almost simultaneously founded the Coaches Training Institute. Both organizations quickly began graduating trained coaches who entered private practice as well as corporate settings. In 1996, only 200 people attended the first International Coach Federation (ICF) conference. Attendance increased to 300 by 1997. From these modest numbers, who could have anticipated that the ICF would include 14,000 members worldwide by 2005? Nearly 50 training programs currently prepare professional coaches both within the United States and around the world. (Williams & Davis 2002).

Also beginning in the mid-1990s, references to executive and corporate coaching expanded into an endless cascade of books and articles. From Robert Hargrove's

Masterful Coaching (2003) to William Hendricks' *Coaching, Mentoring, and Managing: Breakthrough Strategies to Solve Performance Problems* (1996), authors have been producing a steady stream of fieldbooks and textbooks on corporate coaching.

Coaching, as Myles Mace observed 50 years ago, had always been a special perk for corporate executives. As the twenty-first century begins, coaching has now become generally available to everyone. Coaches have carved out specialty niches unknown even a few years ago. These niches range from life coaching to relationship coaching, from diet management to retirement planning. Coaches will help you organize your office or your household closets. Some of these specialty niches have developed to serve pastors, Christian educators, church planters, and redevelopment specialists.

Interest in coaching has blossomed into a multi-million dollar enterprise that spans the globe. Coaching is a hot topic. Pastors, congregations, and church governing bodies cannot ignore crucial questions about how, when, and for whom coaching may be an important leverage point in church transformation.

Why Now?

A number of factors and trends have contributed to coaching's current popularity.

From Structural Redesign to Personal Transformation

During the 1970s and 1980s, most efforts to implement large-scale organizational change ended in frustration and failure. By the early 1990s, many change agents had become disillusioned with structural redesign initiatives and detailed strategic planning. Their hopes now shifted to a newly emerging strategy for organizational change. This strategy focused on the personal and professional transformation of key leaders within organizations. These leaders would then become the leverage points for long-term corporate change. Organizational change increasingly hinged on the transformation of key leaders rather than on structural redesign or the politics of strategic planning.

Two principles undergirded this new approach to organizational change. First, individuals who are personally unwilling to change cannot lead organizational transformation, as Robert Quinn observed in his book, *Deep Change* (1996). Organizational transformation almost inevitably fails when top leaders refuse to alter their own behavior while simultaneously demanding that others within the organization change their attitudes, skills, and behavior. It is difficult to insist that others remove the speck from their eye when you refuse to withdraw the log from your eye. Furthermore, the only persons over whom even the most powerful executives ultimately have any control are themselves. The idea that they can make others change without fundamentally changing themselves is a seriously flawed belief. Such a belief denies the systemic and relational character of human existence. Organizational change begins when leaders accept the challenge of deep personal change.

Second, when leaders take a personal stand to change themselves and how they lead, they automatically initiate powerful changes in the larger organizational environment around them. To change one part of a system is to change the whole system. And the most available and potent leverage point for change is the executive's own behavior and thinking. Leaders occupy a unique social location within organizations. Therefore, when they change themselves, their actions have a ripple effect throughout the whole organization.

Stephen Covey's *Seven Habits of Highly Effective People* (1989) symbolizes this shift from the structural redesign of organizations to the personal transformation of leaders, as does Robert Quinn's *Deep Change*. The popularity of Edwin Friedman (1985, 1999) highlights this same refocusing of change efforts onto the personal transformation of leaders as opposed to corporate restructuring and rational planning.

From the late-1960s until the mid-1980s, many mainline denominations likewise sought renewal through large-scale organizational redesign or strategic planning initiatives. Taking their cues from denominational offices, local congregations adopted these same approaches. Few projects actually achieved their planners' envisioned outcomes, however. The 1990s consequently saw a gradual disillusionment with structural redesign and rational planning across most denominations. Change agents instead turned to the new technologies of personal transformation. If leaders themselves could change, then significant organizational change would follow almost inevitably.

Like their corporate counterparts, denominations began to invest heavily in leader development as their primary strategy for church transformation. In the mid-1990s, the Illinois Great Rivers Annual Conference—where I served as Director of Connectional Ministries—abolished its former Conference Council on Ministries and replaced it with an Academy for Servant Leadership. This Academy was to focus almost exclusively on leader development. Developing and transforming leaders was seen as the key to local church and annual conference transformation.

But changing a leader's lifelong habits, behavior patterns, and mental assumptions is very difficult work. Attending a few weekend workshops will seldom result in substantive change. Deeply engrained, lifelong patterns are hard to alter. Many leaders quickly discovered that personal change was ultimately much more arduous and complex than even organizational redesign or the politics of strategic planning.

Church leaders could learn new vocabulary and describe new approaches to ministry. But their previous theories-in-action frequently remained intact. Advocates of leader development gradually realized that leaders were best able to make significant personal changes when they had someone who could serve as a personal learning consultant and thinking partner—a coach. Leaders might return from one-day seminars enthusiastic about new possibilities, but without a coach to provide support and accountability, momentum and excitement were difficult to maintain.

Ongoing coaching has a more powerful, long-term effect than merely attending a few workshops and then returning home with no support for new ways of thinking or behaving. Long after seminars end and workshop notebooks gather dust, coaches can help leaders address the day-to-day challenges of altering how they think, feel, and act. Coaches can offer support and accountability for a quality of reflective practice that leads to significant personal and organizational transformation.

Coaching emerged when organizational change was re-conceptualized as an inside-out rather than an outside-in process. Large-scale organizational change cannot be managed and planned. It requires leaders who are committed to their own ongoing personal transformation. Such generative learning is difficult to sustain without the kind of support and accountability that coaching provides.

From Schooling to Learning

Changing oneself from the inside out is difficult work. It does not happen overnight. It requires sustained attention and honest commitment to reflective practice and lifelong learning. These characteristics underscore yet another factor that has propelled coaching onto the leadership and organizational change agenda.

Until recently, our society compartmentalized learning and working into two separate boxes. Learning happened in school, generally when we were between the ages of five and eighteen. Adults then applied in the world of work what they had learned as schoolchildren. This model functioned relatively well so long as society changed slowly and technological innovation was incremental and gradual. What my father learned in his rural, one-room schoolhouse did, in fact, sustain him across most of his working life as a farmer.

Those days are gone forever. Rapid, unpredictable change means that learning is now a way of being. We have become a society of lifelong learners. Lifelong learning entails a shift from the passive consumption of information to the active construction of meaning. Learning in the future tense recognizes that adults must learn continually. The rate of learning must now equal or exceed the rate of change if one is to survive, let alone thrive.

For most leaders, lifelong learning entails more than attending a few workshops, retreats, or seminars. Lifelong learning occurs when leaders continually reflect on their leadership practices in ways that build momentum toward important goals and simultaneously deepen their own understanding of themselves and their environment. Such practices are difficult to master—let alone sustain—without ongoing support and accountability. Learning is essentially a social practice. Most of us do not learn effectively in isolation. We learn best when we engage with others in ongoing engagement, conversation, confrontation, and mutual exploration. We create new knowledge through shared action and reflection.

For this reason, coaching has emerged as a significant strategy for leader development. Coaching is a process of shared discovery and generative learning. Coaches support leaders as they uncover their blind spots and explore new ways of thinking, feeling, and acting. They help leaders stay focused on steps that lead to the accomplishment of important ministry goals. In a world where everyone is learning at the speed of change, coaches play an indispensable role in leader development and organizational change. To have a coach is to have a personal learning consultant.

To have arrived at a position of significant church leadership, one must already have mastered many disciplines and skills. But how do top performers learn to do still better? If you are a world-class athlete or actress, you cannot achieve the next level of performance by attending a workshop or enrolling in a class. Tiger Woods cannot improve his golf game by taking a golfing seminar, not even one taught by a skilled professional. The next higher level of performance cannot be taught. It can only be learned. So Tiger Woods turns to Butch Harmon, a golfing coach. Harmon did not "teach" Tiger Woods in the traditional, classroom sense. He instead helped Woods learn what was and what was not working. He increased Woods' capacity as a reflective practitioner. He held Woods accountable for self-chosen commitments to new behavior.

Many leaders—especially those committed to learning as a way of being—are discovering they cannot improve their practice of leadership simply by reading another book or enrolling in another workshop. The next higher level of performance toward which they aspire cannot be taught, it can only be learned. In order to grow faster and go farther, they need a personal learning consultant—a coach.

From Techniques to Core Values

The speed of change contributes to coaching's importance for yet another reason: The more rapid the pace of change, the less important specific tools and techniques become. Tools and techniques come and go. Values, on the other hand, transcend particular trends and fads. Values, from a biblical perspective, are not about what we do or believe. Values are who we are. Our core values are what anchor us to firm ground in times of turbulent, unpredictable change. If the speed of change causes us to lose sight of who we are, then we have lost our very souls. When leaders are not anchored firmly in their own values, they are endlessly buffeted and blown off-course by the latest trend or fad.

The ever-increasing speed of change demands that leaders be anchored firmly in their own values and life purposes. Otherwise they will be blown about by every rumor, trend, or fashion. Ultimately it is the set of the soul that determines the goal and not the calm or the strife.

Gaining clarity about our values is not a simple, straightforward task, however. We hold more than one value simultaneously. Sometimes our values collide and conflict. Some people commit themselves to making choices in light of their values. Others respond to external forces and immediate requests without much awareness of how their decisions affirm or deny their deepest values.

Coaching focuses people on their core values. One important coaching task is values clarification. Coaches guide clients in clarifying their values because they know powerful decisions arise from choices congruent with one's core values. Coaching assists leaders as they invent a personal and organizational future congruent with who they know themselves to be as children of God. Coaching enables people to clarify their values and life purposes so their lives can embody the gospel in a volatile and turbulent world.

With effective coaching, leaders can uncover their blind spots and act more intentionally amid rapidly changing circumstances. Coaching is especially important at those crucial transitional moments when opportunities outnumber resources, when tough choices must be made, or when the link between present behaviors and desired outcomes is unclear.

As the speed of change constantly accelerates, the ability to remain grounded in our core gospel values becomes increasingly important. As leaders find themselves swept up in the unpredictable currents of technological and cultural change, coaching offers them a framework for reflecting on the values that guide their choosing and acting.

Downsizing and the Elimination of Informal Coaching Roles

Technological and societal changes are not the only forces contributing to coaching's popularity. Specific organizational changes have also helped set the stage for coaching's emergence. Corporate downsizing, in particular, has played a significant role in coaching's rise to prominence.

Some forms of coaching have always existed. The apprentice working with a master mechanic, for example, benefited from a time-honored form of coaching. Many seminary graduates became associate pastors who received coaching from the heads of staff with whom they worked. In most organizations, middle managers once served as coaches to the employees beneath them. These middle managers fostered learning, guided people toward new skills, and assisted with career planning and development.

Corporate downsizing has now eliminated most of these informal coaches. As organizations shed layers of middle management, they created a coaching void. Since nature abhors a vacuum, a host of self-employed coaches, trainers, and consultants have rushed to fill this void.

Church systems too have seen a gradual shedding of their middle managers. Most judicatories have significantly smaller staffs than a generation ago. Staff members who once functioned as informal coaches to pastors and church leaders now have neither the time nor the energy for such tasks. Consequently, pastors are inviting external coaches to help them with everything from preaching to congregational redevelopment.

I recently served as the Director of Connectional Ministries in the Illinois Great Rivers Annual Conference of The United Methodist Church. While we still employed a conference staff that included everyone from youth specialists to church growth consultants, the over-all staff was smaller than it had been ten years earlier. Successive financial crises and a changing philosophy about the role of church governing bodies had downsized this staff.

The earlier, larger conference staff had performed more functions than their job descriptions revealed. As I listened to congregations and pastors, I discovered that conference staff members had been informal coaches to many church leaders regardless of their official portfolio. They had fostered learning, anchored new skills, guided people toward possible learning opportunities, and encouraged career planning and development.

Downsizing the conference staff created a coaching void. With staff members no longer available to provide coaching, church leaders were looking elsewhere for these important services. Is it any wonder that some judicatories now propose creating a "culture of coaching" and adopt budgets for new church development or congregational transformation that include funding for coaching contracts?

Disillusionment with Counseling and Managed Care

Changes in the health and insurance industries are another large-scale social change that has contributed to the rise of coaching. As counseling has moved into the realm of managed care, some counselors have become increasingly dissatisfied with the constraints created by insurance regulations and government policies. They have therefore opted to shift from counseling to coaching.

Books such as *Therapist as Life Coach* by Williams and Davis (2002) and *The New Private Practice: Therapist-Coaches Share Stories, Strategies, and Advice* by Grodzki (2002) are explicitly written for people wishing to make a transition from counseling to coaching.

But What Is Coaching, Anyway?

As coaching has grown in popularity, the meaning of the term has become misunderstood and sometimes misused. References to coaching are everywhere. But are all these people and groups describing the same thing?

What, after all, is coaching? What does a coach actually do? What defines coaching and distinguishes it from other, already well-established practices like consulting, counseling, mentoring, and spiritual direction? Is coaching truly a new type of helping relationship? Or is it just putting a new title on the same old thing that consultants and counselors have always been doing?

If coaching has become one more strategy in the toolkit for congregational or organizational transformation, when is it appropriate? Who can benefit? What are its limitations? When, for example, do pastors seek out a coach and when do they confer with a consultant? What unique skill set or toolkit does a coach have?

Questions about coaching are not limited to practical concerns. Coaching has theological implications as well as practical ones. Where does coaching fit within the Christian tradition of leadership and ministry? For coaching to realize its full potential in the church's life and ministry requires shared reflection on these concerns and issues.

CHAPTER TWO

THE COACH: FROM TRANSPORTATION TO TRANSFORMATION

Some church leaders have enthusiastically embraced coaching. Others remain skeptical. Critics complain that the terms *coach* and *coaching* carry a heavy load of negative baggage. The terms conjure up a red-faced sports coach (usually male) shouting orders from the sideline to puppet-like players on the field. Coaching's athletic connotations give it a competitive, hard edge. They imply something masculine, authoritarian, and hierarchical.

Others suggest that coaching is just another fad that will disappear in a few years, as have similar trends and passing fashions the church has previously embraced. They imply coaching is not really a new or distinct helping relationship. It is just putting a new label on the same old thing that consultants and counselors have always done. Among this same group of critics, some equate coaching with giving advice or making helpful suggestions. They wonder what all the fuss is about. People have always been giving advice to their colleagues. So why suddenly dress it up with the title of coaching?

Still other critics find the words *coach* and *coaching* too vague or general. Coaching is used in multiple ways to mean different things, they observe. Sometimes it describes a supervisor's responsibility for developing subordinates. People frequently conflate coaching and mentoring, using the two terms interchangeably. In still other situations, coaching is a remedial activity that happens as the last step before dismissal.

So what specifically does a coach do?

From Carriage to Coach

To establish a working definition of coaching, the best place to begin is with the word itself. The English word *coach* first appeared in the sixteenth century. According to the *Oxford English Dictionary*, it referred to a closed, horse-drawn carriage with seats on the interior for passengers and exterior seats for the coachmen or drivers (1987). It was derived from the French word *coche*, which was a corrupted version of the Hungarian term *koczi szeker*—a wagon from the Hungarian town of Kocs.

So how did we get from a sixteenth-century Hungarian wagon to a twenty-first-century helping relationship? The connection is actually rather obvious: A carriage moves people from one place to another; and so does a helping relationship. A carriage or coach could serve as a vivid metaphor for helping people get from one point to another in their life journeys.

By the middle of the nineteenth century, English universities were describing a private tutor who prepared candidates for examination as a "coach." Coaches at Oxford or Cambridge worked in individualized settings to foster learning and insight. People had also begun using the word *coach* to describe those who trained students for athletic contests. By the end of the nineteenth century, the word *coach* had already become identified with contemporary coaching's two primarily outcomes: learning and performance.

As automobiles replaced carriages in the early twentieth century, the earlier connection between coaches and horse-drawn transportation quickly faded. People thought of a coach only as a person, not a vehicle. *Coach* thus completed its evolution from a form of transportation to a means of transformation.

At its most basic level, coaching is an individualized relationship that helps people go from where they are to where they want to be in their lives through learning and improved performance.

Coaching is not a remedial activity for those who are ineffective. In fact, it seldom works to impose coaching as a disciplinary step or as a last ditch effort to avert an employee's dismissal. The coaching relationship is for leaders who are already functioning well and possess a good grasp of who they are and what they want from life. Good candidates for coaching are psychologically healthy but want to reach higher levels of performance and accomplishment. Coaching is not about fixing what is wrong in a person's ministry or leadership. It involves bringing out extraordinary gifts in the people whom God calls to ministry and mission.

This broad definition of coaching contains several specific qualities and characteristics. Coaching:

- Calls people forth to larger purposes
- Increases people's awareness and self-responsibility
- Encourages accountability for responsible action
- Empowers people to link inner purpose with outer work
- Is a mutual partnership
- Adds value to organizations and individuals

Figure 2.1 What Coaches Do

Coaching Is an Evocative Relationship

The measure of a coach's effectiveness always remains indirect. On a playing field, the coach does not make the touchdown or score the run. An actor's voice coach seldom appears in the footlights or receives the audience's applause. In Christian congregations, the coach is not the one who delivers the sermon or teaches children in a Sunday school classroom. His or her impact is always indirect, mediated through the client's own accomplishments and insights.

Effective coaching is therefore evocative. Good coaches call forth or evoke their clients' best gifts and truest selves. Supervisors plan, direct, and control. Teachers impart wisdom or instruct. Friends or neighbors give advice and make suggestions. Coaches, on the other hand, call forth the best in others

Try as he might to ignore his vocation, the prophet Jeremiah could not silence God's voice calling him forth, "Before I formed you in the womb I knew you, and before you were born I consecrated you; I appointed you a prophet to the nations." (Jer 1:5) Isaiah was in the Temple offering sacrifices when the Spirit called him forth to be a prophet and touched his lips with burning coals. (Isa 6:1-8) Amos was a dresser of sycamore trees and herdsman when God summoned him to speak a word of judgment against the northern kingdom of Israel. (Amos 7:14) Jesus called out Peter, James, and John from repairing their nets and they followed him.

Prophets and apostles encountered someone or something that evoked from them a life-changing vocational call. Good coaching creates an opportunity for people to listen to the same life-changing Spirit calling them forth to their ministries. It provides a setting where people can equip themselves for these ministries by clarifying goals, making commitments, and holding themselves accountable for their promises.

People easily lose sight of their larger purposes and visions. Daily circumstances distract them. Other voices tell them what they cannot do and what abilities they lack. These voices remind people of their failures or the impossible obstacles they face. These voices are the internalized messages of family or friends or bosses who have told them what they "should" do or who they "ought" to be. They tempt people to adopt easy goals. They entice them to abandon the big vocations to which God may be calling them.

Yet people always yearn to act on what matters most in life. They want to know they are spending their energy and attention on something that makes a difference. People intuitively sense that they have yielded too easily to the practical, the popular, and the easily achieved goals that their culture or its internalized voices set before them. They hunger for a place where they can listen deeply to the divine voice that calls forth their truest selves and evokes their deepest commitments.

Good coaching enables people to hear the Holy Spirit, who is continually calling people forth to their authentic vocations. The coaching relationship creates a place where people can connect back to what really matters, to what they value most deeply, to what evokes their highest calling.

Coaching temporarily suspends the immediate pressures of work and action so individuals can think about themselves and their lives in a safe, hospitable space. It breaks the cycle of reaction and repetition so people can reflect on their lives. Most people are easily sucked into the vortex of daily circumstances where they find it difficult to stay focused on who they authentically want to be and what they genuinely want to do. Coaching helps clients stay focused on the larger visions to which God is calling them rather than yield to the old inner voices, the tired daily routines, or the immediate pressures of work.

Coaching is evocative because it connects people to God's big agenda for their lives—an agenda that calls forth their best gifts and deepest wisdom. Coaches do not let people settle for second best. They hold God's vision for their clients when clients want to get lost in smaller agendas of easy goals and simple answers. Even when people fail to believe in their own gifts, their coaches believe in them and seek to create a safe, inviting space where they can reconnect to a better way and a higher gift.

Coaches Increase Self-Awareness and Self-Responsibility

Coaches help clients become more aware of their own thoughts, feelings, and unspoken patterns of behavior. People can take responsibility for significant personal transformation only when they are aware of how their own behaviors and thoughts are getting in the way of what they want from life. Without an awareness of their own complicity in their situations, people find it too easy to place the responsibility for change on other people. The great temptation is to blame others and say they should be the ones to change. Yet the only person anyone ever has the ability to change is oneself.

So long as I remain unaware of my own collusion in the circumstances that hold me back, I am tempted to pray for the Holy Spirit to change "those others" who are causing bad things to happen to me. What I should pray for, however, is the Spirit's transformation of those areas of my life that hinder my own best intentions. Until I am aware of how I contribute to unwanted results, I am not likely to take responsibility for collaborating with the Spirit in addressing these behaviors. Awareness and self-responsibility are closely related.

Coaching Heightens People's Awareness of Themselves and Their Behavior

Most people hug the shoreline of their experience. They skim life's surface, unaware of the meaning or consequences of their thoughts, feelings, and behaviors. When people operate on autopilot, they lose touch with their authentic selves. They live superficially, shaped by other people's opinions or by outside events.

The call to the Christian life includes the expectation that we will awake from our slumbers and open our eyes. "For everything that becomes visible is light. Therefore it says, 'Sleeper, awake! Rise from the dead, and Christ will shine on you.' Be careful then how you live, not as unwise people but as wise." (Eph 5:14-15)

According to John's Gospel, it is within the concrete particularities of human experience that the eternal Word dwells. "And the Word became flesh and lived among us, and we have seen his glory, the glory as of a father's only son, full of grace and truth." (John 1:14) Where do people look for God? God comes to them and abides with them in the flesh-and-blood experiences of human existence. People see God's glory in their daily experience.

Yet people seldom tune their awareness to this, their actual lived experience. "It is not in heaven, that you should say, 'who will go up to heaven for us, and get it for us so that we may hear it and observe it?' Neither is it beyond the sea that you should say, 'Who will cross to the other side of the sea for us, and get it for us so that we may hear it and observe it?' No, the word is very near to you; it is in your mouth and in your heart for you to observe." (Deut 30:12-14)

So long as people skim the surface of their awareness, they fail to listen to the still, small voice of God. This voice arises from deep within human experience. Unless our awareness is tuned to its quiet tones and subtle sounds, we miss the Spirit's invitation to participate in God's mission to our world. People hear God's voice calling them forth only when they stop sleepwalking through life.

Coaching supports people who want to live more purposefully. It increases people's awareness of what they are experiencing and thinking so they can listen for God's power, presence, and purpose in their lives. It offers people a relational space where they can listen to their own hearts and recover an awareness of their deepest need for meaningful action. Coaching is for people who want to deepen their awareness of what God really wants them to create in their lives and the world.

When people lack awareness of their own experience, they are also blind to how their thinking or behavior gets in the way of what they really want from life. Sometimes what we hope to achieve is sabotaged by our assumptions about who we are or what we can achieve. The Sunday school teacher who wants children to attend her class scolds them for their absences when they finally do come. She thus ensures they associate coming to Sunday school with feeling bad about themselves. The church planter substitutes keeping busy for being clear about priorities, thus depriving himself of the very clarity of purpose most needed to organize a new faith community. Coaching offers an opportunity for people to reflect on and alter the unexamined thoughts and behaviors that keep them from getting the results they want.

Coaching also provides a setting where people can become more aware of the ways they talk themselves out of what they already know to be true. People are prone to be confused about what they really want from life. They confuse their wants and their needs. They desire conflicting things. They substitute other people's expectations of them for their own inner sense of purpose. Over time, the clarity of even a sharply focused vision begins to blur. People need some safe setting where they can examine their own fuzzy thinking and confused priorities. People can take greater responsibility for staying focused and living a purposeful life when they become more aware of how they talk themselves out of what they know and want.

Coaches do not give advice or provide expert analysis. They ask questions that invite clients to explore their own thinking and behavior. As clients explore their thoughts and assumptions, they become more aware of their own true values. They recognize how they inadvertently sabotage their own goals. Asking questions is one of the best ways that coaches can stop superficial, presumptive thinking. A good question stops people in their tracks. They are suddenly paying attention. They stop and observe what is going on. A good question jolts people into awareness.

On the other hand, nothing kills people's awareness like advice, expert instruction, or criticism. When someone tells people what their own experience "should" mean, they are taught not to pay attention to their own intuitive awareness. When someone tells people what they "ought" to do, they are taken out of their own immediate awareness of the situation and directed to someone else's opinion or perception. Good coaches do not give advice. They are not the "sage on the stage" giving expert opinions. They are instead the "guide on the side" who asks questions to heighten a client's awareness of his or her own assumptive thinking and its unintended consequences.

Increased Awareness Leads to Increased Responsibility

Increasing awareness is important because awareness and responsibility are closely intertwined. People cannot take responsibility for something until they are aware of it. Once they are genuinely aware of something, their responsibility toward it becomes unavoidable. Just telling people to be responsible does not necessarily make them feel responsible. This dynamic explains why advice and direct instruction rarely change performance.

A few years ago, my sons played in the local recreation department's sports program. They were on different teams and had two different coaches. Our older son's coach was an expert in the game. He told the children what they were to do. During weekly practice sessions, he would carefully instruct them on how to run, kick, or block. Then, during games, he would yell at his players as they ran up and down the field, "Get over there and kick that ball." He would shout from the sidelines, "Kick it! Kick it with your right foot!" Or he would scream at them, "What's wrong with you? Start running. Don't just stand there." It was what I typically expected from a sports coach and it definitely did not motivate most of the players. In spite of his telling them to take responsibility for the ball, most players would just stand there or make a half-hearted effort to run and kick as he had told them to do.

Our other son had a different coach. This coach seldom raised his voice. He almost never criticized what they were doing. Instead, he would ask them questions. "How did your leg feel when you tried to kick the ball that way?" Or, "When you are running toward the ball and getting ready to kick, which way is the ball spinning? Once he asked my son, "When you were running to the left of the field on that last play, what were you thinking would happen?" His questions were designed to increase players' awareness of the intentions behind their actions as well as the actual outcomes their actions produced. Amazingly, his players outperformed the other team with the more expert coach.

Why? This coach saw the connection between increasing awareness and developing responsibility. When he heightened his players' self-awareness, he automatically intensified their sense of responsibility for what they were doing. Good coaching is not about instructing, telling, teaching, advising, or critiquing. Coaches instead ask powerful questions that heighten their clients' awareness. From this place of heightened awareness, people can take fuller responsibility for the spiritual gifts with which God has gifted them.

People come to coaching so that they can take more responsibility for their own gifted lives rather than drift along at the whim of events, other people, or even their own past choices. They want to live more intentionally in harmony with their vocational call, their higher purposes, and their core values. But coaches cannot release clients to take this quality of responsibility for their own lives when they simply tell them what to do. People who give advice or take on the role of experts actually disempower others. Coaches heighten people's awareness of their own thinking and its consequences so they can take responsibility for their actions and circumstances.

Coaches Build Accountability for Responsible Action

Acting responsibly means being accountable for the commitments we make. People deny God's desired future for themselves when they say, "It doesn't matter. I'll be happy with whatever happens." Such responses are never genuinely truthful. Outcomes do matter. When people respond, "It doesn't matter," they are usually trying to find a polite way to avoid the accountability conversation:

- What are you planning to do about what genuinely matters to you?
- By when?
- How will I know?

Coaching is an action-oriented discipline that helps people stay focused on and accountable for the results they want to achieve.

Accountability serves as a measuring rod for how we are growing toward the love, knowledge, and service of both God and neighbor. Being accountable means taking seriously the human freedom with which God has gifted us. Coaches help people move beyond lip service to what matters most in their lives. They help clients clarify and then be accountable for actions that make visible their commitments, values, and God-given purposes in life.

Each week, the congregation where our family worships begins its Sunday service with an act of confession and assurance of forgiveness. This liturgical action reminds us of the values and purposes to which we have committed ourselves in our baptisms. It affirms our accountability to God and each other for how we live out these commitments. Ultimately we are the commitments we make. If coaches did nothing more than hold clients accountable for the commitments they make, they would have a huge impact on people's lives.

Jesus tells a parable about a landowner who left for an extended period of time and entrusted his servants with his property. To one he left one talent; to another, three talents; and to a third, ten talents. When he returned, he came and settled his accounts. He demanded an accounting of how each had acted on his commitment. (Matt 25:14-30) Immediately after this parable of the talents, Matthew's gospel unfolds the judgment of the nations. The Son of Man returns, sits on the throne, and receives an accounting of all peoples: "Truly I tell you, just as you did it to one of the least of these who are members of my family, you did it to me." (Matt 25:40)

Matthew concludes his gospel's last block of Jesus' teachings with these parables about accountability. He seems to be suggesting that authentic faith involves not just pious thoughts and warm hearts. It also includes concrete actions for which the Son of Man will hold Christians accountable. People are accountable for actually living the lives to which they have committed themselves in their baptisms.

Paul writes to the Corinthian church that everyone will be held accountable for their work: "According to the grace given to me, like a skilled master builder I laid a foundation, and someone else is building on it. Each builder must choose with care how to build on it . . . the work of each builder will become visible, for the Day will disclose it, because it will be revealed with fire, and the fire will test what sort of work each has done . . . Do you not know that you are God's temple and that God's Spirit dwells in you?" (1 Cor 2:10,13,16)

Both Paul and Matthew highlight the accountability conversation.

- To what purposes and values have you publicly committed yourselves?
- By when will you act on them?
- How will others know what you have done?

Unfortunately, accountability has a bad reputation. As children, we were held accountable for cleaning our rooms or doing our chores. Teachers held us accountable for turning in our homework. In the name of accountability, parents and other authority figures pestered and badgered us about tasks they wanted us to do.

People sometimes use accountability as a blunt instrument with which to threaten others. "I'm going to hold you accountable for this," a supervisor warns her subordinate. "You're accountable to me for these piano lessons," parents say menacingly to their children. This kind of accountability usually involves someone else's agenda. It is seldom about our own plans and choices. Someone else is holding us accountable for what they want us to be or do.

Accountability actually means something quite different. The English word *accountability* comes from a Latin word meaning "to stand freely and be counted." The Latin word referred to a voting process in the ancient Roman Senate. Senators stood and literally walked across the senate chamber to cast their affirming vote for a measure. This act of walking across the floor demonstrated the stand they were taking. It embodied the commitment they were making to carry out the measure if it passed.

Accountability is about taking a stand for something that matters deeply to us and to which we are committed. When people are accountable, they declare where they stand and what they are going to do. People are more likely to follow through on a particular action if they tell a friend or associate about their intentions. The likelihood of their actually doing something increases as they share their commitments with others and enlist their support. The coaching relationship represents one arena where people can declare their intentions and enlist support.

Accountability also means seeking feedback on one's progress toward publicly stated goals or purposes. If people are truly committed to particular actions, then they will seek feedback on their progress. Feedback helps people adjust their actions or goals in light of the actual results they are getting. The coaching relationship gives people a safe place to reflect on feedback.

For coaches and clients, accountability is not about scolding, judging, or nagging. It means asking clients to give an account of how they are living out the commitments they have publicly declared. Accountability involves seeking and monitoring feedback on one's own progress or lack of progress toward one's goals. In the coaching relationship, clients take a stand for what matters in their lives. Their coaches help them design structures that preserve personal accountability for acting on these commitments.

When people move from living habitually to living intentionally, they enter new territory. Existing structures and relationships will try to pull them back into old ways of acting and thinking. Jesus tells a perceptive parable about this pull of old habits and behaviors: "When the unclean spirit has gone out of a person, it wanders through waterless regions looking for a resting place, but not finding any, it says, ' I will return to my house from which I came.' When it comes, it finds it swept and put in order. Then it goes and brings seven other spirits more evil than itself, and they enter and live there; and the last state of that person is worse than the first." (Luke 11:24-26) Coaching serves as a designed alliance that empowers people to resist this pull of old ways and to maintain their forward momentum.

Improving our performance usually comes from making many small, incremental increases in our effectiveness. Accountability within the coaching relationship helps clients stay focused on the few critical variables that lead to such improvements. Accountability in the coaching relationship is about awareness, feedback, and enlisting support for the intentions that clients have declared.

Coaches Link Inner Purpose to Outer Work

Coaching thus oscillates between two poles—inward intention and outer action. People's commitments emerge out of their core values and inner purposes. Coaches help clients identify their most deeply held values and the purposes to which God is calling them. Coaches then provide support and accountability as people make concrete changes in their lives so these values and vocations find fuller expression.

People, the Psalmist says, are like trees planted by streams of living water. Their inner roots reach down into the moist, life-giving soil and their branches reach outward with good fruits (Ps 1:3). People lead holy lives when the outward fruit of their experience is congruent with their most deeply rooted values. In the same way, the apostle James reminds his readers that the inner world of faith and the outer work of action belong together: "What good is it, my brothers and sisters, if you say you have faith but do not have works? . . . So faith by itself, if it has no works, is dead." (Jas 2:14, 17)

Coaches work from the inside out. They are always seeking both to deepen clients' self-understanding and to forward their responsible action in the world. Coaching operates on the principle that action and intention belong together: Action leads to learning and learning to action. Coaches always seek to simultaneously enhance performance and deepen learning.

Coaches work with the inner being of their clients. This inner work entails building resilience, working through resistance to personal change, connecting to core values and beliefs, claiming a vocational call or identity from God. Coaching engages the question of being when it encourages self-reflection and self-awareness. Coaching simultaneously focuses on what clients are actually doing in their lives. Its outer work involves guiding clients toward clear goals, encouraging them to move out of their safety zone and risk failure for the sake of new learning. Coaches hold clients accountable for their performance, responsible action, and concrete results in the world. They help clients move forward by taking concrete steps toward their goals.

Coaches wear bifocal glasses. They are always looking both at clients' inner values and outward behavior, their assumptive thinking and its behavioral consequences. Coaching involves a constant oscillation between the inner and outer. One can never be neglected at the other's expense. Anything done to enhance one must also keep in view its impact upon the other.

Coaching and the Human Developmental Cycle

Whether coaching places its emphasis more on inner purpose or outer work depends, in part, on the stage of life through which clients are passing. Most adults experience life in one of two basic modalities. People are either in a transition or a stable life stage (Levinson 1978). At certain points in our lives we are clear where we are going and fully claim our life path. At other times, we pause at resting places to renew ourselves. We re-orient ourselves around a new vision of God's call and claim upon our lives.

Transitional and stable stages repeat themselves across the human lifespan. (See Figure 2.2) Stable stages are usually times of Engagement with life's tasks and responsibilities. The transitional stages are occasions for Self-Renewal through withdrawal and introspection.

During the stable stage of Engagement, people are upbeat, energetic, and focused. They experience life as providing a reliable flow of energy and opportunities. They are clear about who they are, what they want from life, and where their lives are heading. During this stage, people are more outwardly focused. They build upon and extend the platforms they have constructed in the preceding transitional stage.

The Engagement Stage has two substages: A "Building the Future" substage when people are moving confidently toward new goals and purposes, and a "Drifting" substage when people are moving with the established momentum of past accomplishments rather than actively creating something new. Both substages focus predominantly on outward doing. Both are marked by setting and attaining clear goals, acquiring new skills, celebrating and giving thanks to God for our accomplishments.

Figure 2.2 Coaching Through Life's Stages and Transitions

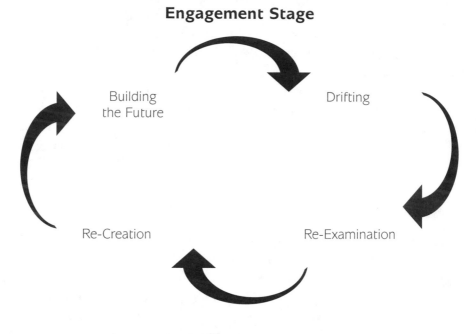

Engagement Stage

Building
the Future

Drifting

Re-Creation

Re-Examination

Self-Renewal Stage

During the transitional Self-Renewal Stage, people's energy drops. They typically turn away from outward doing and are more focused on their inner being. They are less clear who they are or where they are going in life. Experience is chaotic and unfocused. It may even be painful, disrupted, and difficult to endure. People often feel unable to manage their lives in this stage. They disengage and re-evaluate their lives and relationships. Rather than being focused on outward goals and feedback, they are more apt to listen to their inner voices and longings. New clarity of purpose and vision can emerge as the hard-won fruit of a transitional stage.

The transitional stage of Self-Renewal also has two substages. During the substage of Re-Examination, people withdraw and seek new meaning and identities for themselves. Then, in the substage of Re-Creation, people actively acquire the tools, skills, knowledge, and networks for their newly forged purposes. During both these substages, people are inwardly oriented. They seek to understand or develop their inner being.

People who successfully negotiate a transitional stage of Self-Renewal emerge with tremendous energy and focus. They experience life's challenges as positive opportunities to grow and be rewarded. They use this new energy and clarity of purpose as a platform upon which to construct plans and goals that forward the momentum of their lives.

Self-Renewal Substage 1: Re-Examination

People know they have entered the first substage of Self-Renewal when they are no longer satisfied with the status quo of their lives. These feelings eventually reach a breakpoint when they decide to take charge of their situation and stop drifting. They begin to re-examine their goals and values in order to re-establish a firm basis for their lives. This shift propels them into Self-Renewal's first substage: Re-Examination.

As this substage begins, people say good-bye to past goals and life structures. They withdraw from their old world of relationships, accomplishments, and activities. Cut loose from these external moorings, they are free to spend more time in inward reflection. Who are they? What do they really want from life? What do they feel called to be and do? What assumptions and rules have guided them in the past? Are these previous mental models sufficient to give future meaning and purpose to their lives? The substage of Re-Examination is often marked by withdrawal and deep introspection.

Self-Renewal Substage 2 : Re-Creation

People eventually grow tired of cocooning and introspection. They catch a glimpse of some trustworthy vision for their lives, however vague and unclear it still may be. They commit themselves both to this vision and to the knowledge, values, skills, and habits needed for its realization. This emerging vision becomes a stake in the ground to which they tether themselves.

When this happens, they have stepped into the second transitional substage: Re-Creation. During this substage, people acquire the skills, knowledge, and resources to claim fully their new vision. Their energy, which has ebbed low during the previous stage, begins to return. They reach out to others. They seek assistance and support. They move forward with renewed confidence in themselves and their vision.

While some of their energy is focused outwardly, most is still channeled inwardly toward their own growth and development. A Japanese graduate student once told me that the word *kokoro* in Japan refers to perfecting the inner self. To master any discipline is not just a matter of acquiring outward tools and techniques. *Kokoro* means acquiring an inner way of being consistent with one's chosen discipline. *Kokoro* is the developmental task of the substage of Re-Creation.

In North America, people tend to focus primarily on tools and techniques. To produce extraordinary results, however, people must acquire not just a bag of tricks and techniques. Extraordinary results flow from an inner being consistent with people's chosen purposes. Congruence and authenticity, however, do not happen overnight. They take time. During this substage, people acquire the inner disciplines and outer strategies consistent with the renewed vision of their lives or work that God has given to them.

Engagement-Substage 1: Building the Future

As the process of learning and growth gains momentum, people's energy shifts more into outward activity and achievement. People feel fully engaged in achieving their purposes and realizing their values. During this substage of Building the Future, people experience amazing energy and drive. They feel they can accomplish anything. Usually, people recall this period as a time when they were living life to its fullest. They are busy but guided by clear goals. There is a thirst for learning and creative activity.

Engagement-Substage 2 : Drifting

This period of accomplishment eventually begins to level off. The arc of engagement peaks and starts to wane. People experience themselves as having reached a plateau where they are simply coasting on past knowledge, skills, and accomplishments. Gradually they begin to operate on autopilot. Nothing may be externally wrong or troubling; but, inwardly, they feel a drop in energy and a loss of enthusiasm for what they are doing. This experience of coasting on past achievements and skills typifies the substage of Drifting.

At some point, people recognize this inner shift. This recognition serves as a breakpoint that initiates transition into the stage of Self-Renewal. With this shift comes an inward focus on one's own being rather than an outward emphasis on tasks and responsibilities. The whole cycle of engagement and self-renewal thus repeats itself. No set timetable dictates how long each substage in this cycle will take. The timing varies from individual to individual. Some people linger longer or move more quickly through various substages depending on their age, experience, and situation.

Coaching in the Different Stages and Phases
of Human Development

This oscillation between developmental phases of doing and being has enormous implications for coaching.

Transitional stages are optimal moments for coaching. People are more open to new behaviors and responses in such moments. During the Self-Renewal Stage, people are usually more energetic, enthusiastic, and willing to accept challenges. During times of Self-Renewal, people are more aware of themselves and their circumstances. They can more easily discern assumptions that otherwise remain hidden. Coaches play a critical role in helping people maximize their awareness and self-understanding during these periods of Self-Renewal.

Coaching plays a different role in the Engagement Stage. While the inner work of values and vision are still important, more emphasis can be placed on outward disciplines that help clients grow faster and go farther. Clients sharpen their goal setting and problem solving skills. They increase the speed, accuracy, and accountability of their decision making.

Coaches must match their own activities to the needs of their client's developmental life stage. When there is a mismatch between the coaching emphasis and the client's developmental needs, both coach and client experience frustration.

For example, during the Building the Future substage, clients feel confident, energized, and courageous. They are willing to take risks and follow their own sense of purpose. The results they seek from coaching include setting high goals and achieving them, feeling their own power, enjoying the full engagement of their skills and gifts. An effective coach will aid clients in networking, pacing, and goal-setting. Coaches may give special attention to clients' time management and celebration of accomplishments.

A coaching approach that emphasized deep introspection would be out of sync with these clients' developmental needs. An activity very appropriate for the Re-Examination substage of Self-Renewal, for instance, would neither enhance clients' forward momentum toward significant action nor deepen their knowledge of self.

Conversely, the client who has taken the first steps toward self-renewal is not well-served by coaching that seeks to optimize doing. This client benefits from coaching that encourages introspection, journaling, meditation, or other reflective practices. Coaching that emphasized time management, maintaining focus, planning, or goal-setting could actually distract clients from the developmental tasks necessary for their own self-renewal.

Later, as this client enters the Re-Creation substage of Self-Renewal, the coach can help her think through activities where new skills can be acquired, new personal or professional networks developed, and needed knowledge gained. Coaches best serve their clients during this period when they help them clarify their purposes, grow increasingly confident of their vocational call, and claim their new-found identity.

Similarly, the Building the Future substage is one of full engagement. The coach works to give the client full permission to have the impact he or she wants.

This is not a time for coaches to invite clients to create exit plans from what they are doing. This period is not when coaches encourage their clients to question their goals, purposes, and values.

Coaching strategies appropriate for the Drifting substage help clients name their emptiness and uncertainty. The coaching relationship can create a safe space where clients acknowledge what they are truly feeling about themselves and their lives. Coaches can encourage clients to claim time for exploring not so much what they are doing but who they are being and who God may be calling them to be.

Good coaching does not mismatch its activities, questions, and purposes to the client's developmental needs. Coaches constantly evaluate and re-assess their clients' developmental needs so they are providing an appropriate holding environment for them. A coach's emphasis is never completely on the client's being and never totally on his or her doing. The coaching session constantly oscillates between a concern for the client's being and doing. But there is a clear shift in amount of attention given to one or the other depending on the client's developmental cycle and immediate needs.

Coaches must be flexible and nimble. Someone once said that a person with a hammer sees everything as a nail. In the same way, inexperienced coaches can sometimes adopt a one-size-fits-all approach to coaching. They assume everyone will benefit from introspection and values clarification. Or they believe that they should immediately help everyone set goals, develop achievable plans, and monitor time management skills. Such coaches are beginning with their own skills, interests, and agendas rather than following the agenda of their clients. Their clients' agendas will arise out of the developmental challenges they are facing.

Coaches are always assessing where the client currently is and what is needed to forward his or her movement into the next developmental stage or phase. Questions that help coaches assess their clients' developmental stage or transition include (See Figure 1.2):

- Does what the client is saying reflect a stable or unstable time in their life?
- What developmental activities do they seem to be engaged in?
- What is happening in their lives that might provide clues about their stage or phase?
- What might be pointing toward movement into the next developmental period?

When people move from one life stage to the next, previously effective habits of thought or well-developed skills can often become barriers to further growth and achievement. What once brought people success now bogs them down. Developmental periods of self-renewal are occasions for people to examine how

Figure 2.3 Developmental Needs and Coaching Activities

Engagement (Focus on "doing")

Building

Developmental Needs	Coaching Activities
Energized and confident in self and goals Challenged to take risks, follow purposes Goal-setting skills Networking skills Learning or acquiring new knowledge and habits Claim successes and purposes	Goal-setting Time management Learning from experience Encouraging the heart Sustaining hope Building resilience Maintaining focus

Drifting

Developmental Needs	Coaching Activities
Sense of decline and plateauing Feeling trapped Sadness and anger	Name the feelings Release anger and sadness Create exit strategy Create space for introspective withdrawal Manage transition from doing to being

Self-Renewal (Focus on "being")

Re-Examination

Developmental Needs	Coaching Activities
Discovery of new purposes Reclaiming of core values Hearing God's vocational call Self-renewal	Meditative practices Deep introspection Exploration of self Listening Encouragement of solitude Exploring or testing-out possibilities

Re-Creation

Developmental Needs	Coaching Activities

Build capacity for new identity or purpose
Clarify values, goals
Increase confidence in self and call
	Channel and focus new-found
	  energy
	Guide toward learning needed skills
	  or knowledge
	Help pace activity, manage transition
	  from being to doing

old rules of thumb or mental assumptions may have become barriers to further achievement and learning. Coaches help their clients uncover these blind spots so that they can move forward more confidently, effectively, and consciously.

Coaches Are Partners in Creating the Life Before God the Client Wants

Coaching is a subtle dance of partnership between coaches and clients. Coach and client are constantly co-creating the relationship based on what clients need in that moment to advance their purposes and goals in a particular phase of their developmental cycle. Coaches follow their clients' agenda rather than imposing their own assumptions and strategies on them. They are partners with their clients.

But coaching is a partnership for other, equally important reasons. Most people are not likely to examine honestly their mental assumptions and ingrained patterns until they feel safe. Clients will not feel comfortable lowering their mental and emotional defenses until they sense they are on a level playing field. They will not risk revealing themselves in the coaching relationship if they feel the coach is in a "one-up" position to judge, scold, or criticize them. To let their guard down and look at themselves truthfully requires a climate of trust and acceptance.

This need for a climate of trust and openness means the coaching relationship is a partnership between equals. Coaching is therefore a helping relationship outside the usual superior-subordinate roles. It is a mutually designed partnership between client and coach. Both parties mutually define what will be given and received in the relationship. Client and coach work together to create a partnership that serves the client's needs. In this partnership, the client is always in control of the direction and the agenda.

The coach is therefore not at the center of the coaching relationship. The coaching relationship is about the client, not the coach. Coaches create holding environments where clients feel safe and secure enough to listen to their own deepest, God-given values and purposes. Coaches do not impose some predetermined goal or cookie-cutter vocation on their clients. They do not attempt to decide what is best for a client and then direct the conversation toward this outcome.

If the relationship has become an arena for the coach to prove how insightful, wise, creative, or competent he or she is, then it has ceased to be a coaching relationship. When coaches are doing all the work in the relationship, then they have ceased to provide effective coaching. The coach's need to solve, to fix, to be right, or to be in control seldom calls forth a client's best gifts.

This is different from consulting, where the consultant comes with specialized knowledge and is expected to speak from a position of expertise. It is different from teaching, where the teacher arrives in the classroom with greater knowledge and preparation than the student. The teacher and consultant both set the agenda for the relationship. Coaching, however, is not about the coach's expertise, wisdom, or pre-packaged programs. It is about partnership.

Theologian Letty Russell (1975) describes partnership as a relationship between equals characterized by sharing, synergy, and serendipity. Because it is a partnership, power resides within the coaching relationship itself, not within the coach. The coach is therefore never in a "one-up" position relative to the client. He or she is not an expert who delivers a pre-packaged program. The coach is instead a partner with the client in designing the kind of relationship that will best serve the client's needs—a relationship where sharing, synergy, and serendipity are all possible.

The apostle Paul certainly had every reason to feel he could operate from a "one-up" position over his churches. After all, he was the one to whom the Risen Christ appeared on the Damascus Road. He was the missionary apostle without whom they might never have existed as congregations. Yet he usually avoids speaking from a position of power over these congregations. Instead, he typically chooses to emphasize mutual partnerships in Christ. In announcing his coming arrival to Roman Christians, for example, Paul writes that he comes not just to bring them the spiritual gifts that he as an apostle possesses. He is coming "rather so that we may be mutually encouraged by each other's faith, both yours and mine." (Rom 1:12)

The Pauline correspondence frequently uses the Greek word *koinonia* to describe such partnerships between equals where sharing, synergy, and serendipity emerge. Although it is usually translated as "fellowship," *koinonia* can also mean "partnership," particularly partnerships in Christ that are catalysts for mission. In his letter to Philemon, for example, Paul describes Philemon as his partner. "So if you consider me your partner (*koinonos*), welcome him as you would welcome me." (Phlm 17) Because they are partners, Paul refuses to command Philemon but rather approaches him as an equal. Philemon is not controlled by Paul but left as a free person, responsible for his own choices. "For this reason, though I am bold enough in Christ to command you to do your duty, yet I would rather appeal to you on the basis of love." (Phlm 8-9)

Coaching is not about the coach's voice being heard in a commanding or demanding manner. It is not about the coach determining what is best and then imposing it on the client. It is about creating a relational space—a partnership between equals—where the Holy Spirit can call forth what God has already planted in the client's heart. Coaches are partners with their clients in creating a hospitable space where they can connect to the deepest center within themselves. From this center, God's Spirit calls forth their truest purposes and highest gifts.

Coaching Adds Value to Organizations as Well as Individuals

Finally, coaching is a strategic process that adds value both to the individual and to the organization. The personalized relationship between coach and client can mislead observers into thinking that coaching is only about improving the individual's performance. In fact, coaching's ultimate goal is the transformative impact clients can have on the systems or communities in which they live and work.

Whenever a coach facilitates an individual leader's improved performance, the whole organization also performs better. The coach who works with Tonya Reynolds is not just interested in helping Tonya become a better Sunday school teacher. He or she also values the creation of a more powerful and faithful climate of teaching and learning. Terri Morgan's coach facilitates her growth and learning as a new church planter both for Terri's sake and for the sake of the missional community God is calling into being through Terri's ministry. When Travis Chalmers coaches a church leader as he or she develops a new ministry, it is not just for the sake of that individual's growth and development. It is to enrich the life of the whole congregation and to broaden its impact on the larger community so that God's purposes are fulfilled more completely in a particular time and place.

Coaching's value is not measured merely by the changes in an individual client's perceptions or behavior. From a missional perspective, coaching equips authentic and powerful leaders who can use fully their spiritual gifts for ministry. Through unleashing these gifts for ministry, congregations and church systems are empowered to serve as signs, instruments, and living parables of God's reign.

Coaching and Ministry

One can easily understand why church leaders would be attracted to such a relationship. Many pastors work in relative isolation. Significant contact with other professional colleagues is often sporadic and episodic. The coaching relationship offers the possibility of ongoing support and guided dialogue around important pastoral issues.

Coaching is particularly helpful when church leaders have multiple projects competing for their attention, when resources are scarce, or when they face tough choices. When are these conditions not the norm for ministry? Church leaders often need help staying focused on the results they want to achieve. Daily circumstances can easily distract them from their major goals, causing them to lose sight of their larger purposes and visions. Coaching can play an invaluable role in helping church leaders maintain focus amid daily pressures and distractions.

These two reasons alone account for coaching's popularity with church planters and redevelopment specialists. These pastors typically face severe isolation and loneliness. They often must make difficult choices about how to allocate scarce resources of time, energy, and money. Coaching can play a pivotal role in helping these church leaders stay focused, healthy, and grounded.

Coaching also has implications for lead pastors in multiple-staff settings. Some church staffs operate on the rancher model: Each member has his or her own turf and everyone else stays out. Others are rigidly hierarchical; and lead pastors exercise considerable control. Heads-of-staff who want to empower other staff members while maintaining reasonable oversight would find coaching tools, techniques, and strategies extremely helpful in their work.

Alan Roxburgh (2000, pp. 147-49) has argued that the North American church's current context requires it to move beyond traditional "lone wolf" understandings of ministry. When multiple cultural, demographic, and technological factors are simultaneously in transition, no single individual has the gifts and graces to lead churches successfully through uncertain times. Our historical context requires plural leadership: Different people with different personalities, skills, and perspectives working together in shared leadership arrangements.

Since few individual congregations can afford a multiple staff with all the necessary competencies, the best answer is some form of collaboration, partnership, and mutual sharing among church leaders within defined geographic areas. Mutual conversation and coordination between these leaders can supplement strengths, illumine previously hidden blind spots, and nurture new skills. Collaboration, dialogue, and mutual support in such an arrangement would inevitably take the form of coaching. Indeed, it is difficult to see how Roxburgh's model could thrive unless all participants shared basic coaching skills and competencies.

Finally, many traditional sources for coaching and mentoring have disappeared. As noted earlier, downsized judicatory staffs have lost most of their capacity for coaching church leaders. Downsizing has also resulted in district superintendents and similar judicatory officials overseeing more churches and pastors. They consequently have less time to coach or mentor other leaders. The superintendent's supervisory responsibilities and appointive power also potentially undermine the coaching dialogue itself. Many pastors need another relationship outside these supervisory lines. Coaching provides one obvious solution.

Finally, leaders multiply leadership. They call forth other leaders around them.

In most congregations and communities, there is more ministry to do than people equipped and sent forth to do it. Coaching becomes a powerful way to equip church leaders for ministry and mission. Many Sunday school teachers feel unsupported and unprepared to teach. Coaching represents one tool for better equipping them. Many well-meaning Christians feel called to ministries of service and compassion. But they are unsure of themselves and their gifts. Congregations that provide coaches for these leaders are fulfilling the biblical mandate to equip the saints for the work of ministry. (Eph 4:12)

CHAPTER THREE

COACHING AS A CHRISTIAN PRACTICE

Christian coaches walk alongside others to help them find and fulfill their deepest vocations. Coaching is a ministry of encouragement. With a coach's encouragement and support, people deepen their learning and extend their effective action in the world. To speak of coaching as an expression of Christian ministry is not to throw holy water on essentially secular tools and techniques. Coaching is not something novel and new. It is not another trend or fad the church has borrowed from a business guru or best-selling consultant. The practice of walking with others to encourage, equip, and challenge them has a long biblical history.

Throughout the Bible, men and women engage in coach-like practices to encourage others in their ministries, hold them accountable, foster insight and learning, or link inner purpose to outer work. The priest Eli, for example, coaches the boy Samuel on how to listen for the voice of God in the temple at Shiloh. (1 Sam 3) The prophet Nathan uses coach-like skills to confront King David after his murder of Uriah the Hittite and marriage to Bathsheba. Rather than directly confront David, Nathan adopts a more indirect and powerful approach. He increases David's awareness of his behavior so he can take moral responsibility for the consequences of his own actions. (2 Sam 12) Elijah walks alongside Elisha, encouraging his prophetic gifts, until Elijah's own mantle eventually falls upon him. (1 Kgs 19–2 Kgs 2). Priscilla and Aquilla gently coach Apollos on how to proclaim the good news of Jesus Christ. (Acts 18)

The Bible also provides examples of how not to encourage or coach others. Job's friends come to advise, lecture, and scold. With friends like these, who needs enemies? They are not so much walking alongside Job as lording it over him. No amount of expert advice or scolding will help Job make sense of his circumstances or guide him toward faithful action. Job does not need expert advice. He needs to listen to the voice speaking from the whirlwind.

One of the clearest examples of coaching in the New Testament is Barnabas. Barnabas was an encourager who played a pivotal role in Paul's ministry and missionary journeys. Paul's letters themselves suggest a theological and practical basis for coaching as a Christian practice. The beginning point for coaching as an ecclesial practice, however, is the sacrament of baptism.

Baptism And The Commitment To Coach And Be Coached

Baptism welcomes us into the body of Christ. Through baptism we are initiated into Christian community and its practices. We are introduced both ritually and symbolically to the disciplines through which we grow into our baptismal promises. One of these disciplines is the practice of mutual partnerships for encouragement, growth, and accountability. Such partnerships serve as the foundation for coaching as an expression of Christian ministry.

A Baptismal Commitment to Walk Alongside Each Other

In the congregation where our family worships, both the candidate and congregation are asked very specific questions during the service of Christian baptism. Prior to receiving baptism, candidates renounce evil and profess their faith in Christ. Having heard this profession of faith, the congregation affirms the faith of the whole church and promises to guide and nurture the newly baptized by word and deed, with love and prayer, encouraging them to love, know, and serve the God made known in Jesus Christ.

This brief promise of guidance, nurture, and encouragement is sandwiched between other, more dramatic parts of the baptismal service. Its significance can easily be overlooked. It lacks the tenderness of an infant being touched with water or the majestic tones of the creed with its ancient cadences. Yet it has far-reaching consequences. This promise is, in fact, the basis for the church's ministry of faith formation. As part of every baptism, the congregation reminds itself of its commitment to encourage, equip, and coach new Christians as they grow in their capacity to love, know, and serve God. This same congregational promise simultaneously reminds the newly baptized that they cannot become Christian alone. They grow in Christ as they walk, work, and love alongside others in the Christian community of faith.

We cannot baptize ourselves. It always takes two people to baptize: One to receive the gift of water and one to give it. Baptism is a sacrament of relationship and connection, of partnership and covenant. For this reason, baptism ordinarily occurs in the context of the community's worship. Baptism reminds believers that they cannot become Christian by themselves. We become Christian only as we give and receive encouragement and support within a covenant community where all members are committed to each person's growth in holiness of heart and witness.

This biblical insistence on covenant and partnership runs counter to much of contemporary culture. Most modern people prefer to think of themselves as rugged individualists. They want to imagine themselves as independent, self-made people. Even active church members sometimes believe that the church community is something extra, added onto their basically private faith. The Christian life cannot be lived without the guidance, support, and challenge of others, however. Coaching represents one expression of our baptismal commitment to such mutual relationships in Christ.

Long-Term Transformation Requires Ongoing Encouragement

Baptism also reminds us that Christian growth and transformation are a lifelong journey. We grow into our baptismal promises. While some conversions may be dramatic and instantaneous, growth toward holiness of heart and life is not an overnight accomplishment. It is a lifelong pilgrimage. Baptism bestows upon us the gift of the Holy Spirit because ongoing sanctification of life requires a power greater than our own.

Coaching as a Christian practice exists to support and sustain the Holy Spirit's ongoing work of sanctification. It represents a grace-filled, accepting relationship where people are set free to look at how their own thinking or behavior may be getting in the way of their becoming the people they already are in God's eyes. Coaching as a Christian practice encourages focused, sustained attention on habitual behaviors or assumptive thinking that hold people back.

Behind our house is a small creek that becomes a raging river after heavy spring rains. Brush and small trees are often carried into the rushing waters. This debris can create logjams as the creek twists and turns its way across our woodlands. It only takes one stuck log to jam the entire flow of debris and trees. In the same way, our lives often become clogged or stuck because one behavior or mental assumption jams up the flow of our lives. One unexamined assumption or self-defeating behavior can create a logjam of unresolved issues.

If our family can cut free the one tree that has created the logjam, then the rest of the debris will typically release itself naturally. We do not need to jiggle free all the logs and trees. Freeing one high leverage log releases the remaining ones. Coaching involves identifying the high leverage changes that will unclog the logjam of our lives. Once this mental or behavioral log has been removed or realigned, others quickly free themselves and we find ourselves back in the flow of life. We discover that the Spirit's life-giving waters can once again move freely within us.

Both coaching and baptism point to the lifelong journey in which we untangle one logjam after another. Disentangled from our own self-limiting behaviors, the living waters of God's Spirit can well up into life-giving rivers of hope and healing. "Let anyone who is thirsty come to me, and let the one who believes in me drink. As the scripture has said, 'out of the believer's heart shall flow rivers of living water.'" (John 4:37b-38)

Here also both baptism and coaching run counter to much of our contemporary culture. We have come to expect instant results. We want an "add water and mix" formula for every difficulty and challenge. We have grown accustomed to the most intractable of difficulties being introduced and resolved in the short space of a one-hour TV drama. Yet significant growth takes much longer and requires deliberate attention and energy. Coaching helps us go faster and move further in disentangling the logjams of unexamined assumptions and unspoken habits that dam up the Spirit's streams of living water.

Togetherness and Building Up One Another in Love

The baptismal commitment to mutual partnerships of encouragement and support arises out of a very specific understanding of Christian community. Coaching and being coached are integral to the New Testament's vision of how we grow up into Christ.

Togetherness and Building One Another Up in Love

A small but often overlooked Greek word sheds important light on how coaching functions as a Christian practice. Signifying togetherness, the Greek word *allelon* is usually translated as "one another" or "each other." It occurs 100 times in the New Testament. Despite its common occurrence, Kittel and Friedrich's ten-volume *Theological Dictionary of the New Testament* does not regard *allelon* as important enough to warrant its own separate entry. The individualist assumptions underlying most modern biblical scholarship have blinded theologians and biblical scholars to the importance of this small word.

Allelon's frequent use in the New Testament reveals how the experience of mutual encouragement was at the heart of early Christian community. Christian service does not emerge in a vacuum. It is not a product of individual effort. Christians are instead co-creators of ministry and mission with God's Spirit and each other. Christian coaching is one way the church makes operational its task of "building up one another in love."

Christians are to "build up each other." (1 Thess 5:11) They are to be "members one of another." (Rom 12:5). They are to "have the same care for one another" (1 Cor 12:25) and "do good to one another and to all." (1 Thess 5:15) The use of *allelon* is particularly significant in John's gospel, where Jesus commands his disciples to love "one another." (John 13:34) John's account of Jesus' washing of the disciples' feet piles one occurrence of *allelon* atop another: "As I have loved you, so you must love one another. By this all men will know that you are my disciples, if you love one another." (NIV John 13:34-35)

New Testament writers regard such mutuality or togetherness as essential for the building up or growth of both the community and the individual. "Let us then pursue what makes for peace and for mutual upbuilding." (Rom 14:19) "Therefore encourage one another and build up each other, as indeed you are doing." (1 Thess 5:11) Similarly, when each member of the body of Christ does his or her part, it "causes the growth of the body for the building up of itself in love." (Eph 4:16).

Jeremiah's call to "build up" Israel

The roots of the New Testament expression "to build each other up in love" lie in the Hebrew Bible, especially in the book of Jeremiah. A frequently repeated theme in the book of Jeremiah is the call to "build up" and "tear down" (Jer 12:14-17, 18:7-9, 24:6, 42:10, and 45:4). Jeremiah's call as a prophet, for example, is to "pluck up" and "build up." (Jer 1:10) The centrality of building up God's people in Jeremiah's prophetic ministry is underscored by his announcement of the new covenant between God and Israel: "The days are surely coming, says the LORD, when . . . just as I have watched over them to pluck up and break down . . . so I will watch over them to build and to plant." (Jer 31:27-28)

God's vineyard Israel has been uprooted by faithlessness and violence. In mercy, God will now replant it and build it up. The prophetic task is not only to deliver God's judgment and to call people to repentance. It is also to build up or cultivate a people of God so God's Reign may blossom in human lives and communities.

Paul's Ministry of Edification or Building Up the Church

Paul understood his own vocation in light of this Old Testament prophetic ministry of "building up" and "tearing down." He tells the Corinthians that he has receive from the Lord power to build up and not to destroy: "So I write these things while I am away from you, so that when I come, I may not have to be severe in using the authority that the Lord has given me for building up and not for tearing down." (2 Cor 13:10)

The Greek word Paul is using in these passages has a dual meaning. We usually translate the Greek words *oikodome* or *oikodomein* as either "build up" or "edify." Building up another for ministry involves learning or edification. But, for Paul, the edification that "builds up" is never just imparting information or abstract knowledge. Knowledge alone does not edify or build up: "Knowledge puffs up, but love builds up" (1 Cor 8:1). Edification happens within covenant relationships where believers walk alongside one another to encourage mutual growth and transformation in Christ. Such edification is neither abstract knowledge or blind technique. It involves what coaching describes as deepening the learning and forwarding the action in people's lives.

The task of "building up" or edifying others is central to how Paul interprets his call as an apostle of Jesus Christ. "Now, even if I boast a little too much of our authority, which the Lord gave for building you up and not for tearing you down, I will not be ashamed of it." (2 Cor 10:8)

When coaches come alongside others to watch over them in love and build them up in Christ, they are engaging in the togetherness (*allelon*) that leads to edification (*oikodomene*). One sure sign of authentic Christian community is the courage to edify or build up others in love. Another is the humility to receive support and encouragement from others. Coaching and being coached are integral to Christian community. When we closely examine the New Testament words *allelon* and *oikodomein,* we discover that they disclose how important co-active or mutual encouragement is to authentic Christian community.

Coaching As Cultivation or Building Up In Love

Coaching is a form of cultivation that seeks to build up or edify others in love so fruitful lives can blossom and bear fruit. The coaching relationship cultivates an interpersonal space where people can be built up, where they can find encouragement to address barriers to growth and ministry.

I grew up on a farm in east central Illinois. Each spring my father planted corn and soybeans in the fields around our home. Farmers, I discovered at a young age, do not make seeds grow. They create the conditions that encourage growth and fruitfulness. Cultivation is not about making something happen. It is about removing the barriers or constraints that prevent a seed's natural tendency toward growth from unfolding.

Every spring, my father would disk and harrow the field before planting. He was removing the natural barrier of hard, compacted soil, which prevented the seed from taking root. Later, he would till the soil to remove weeds from around the growing plants. Otherwise the weeds would sap nutrients from the soil, constraining the emerging plant's growth. He regularly fertilized his fields so the natural constraints of poor minerals or nitrogen were removed. He could never make a seed grow; but he could remove constraints to growth by cultivating conditions where seeds had the best possible encouragement to grow.

Paul, like Jeremiah before him, drew upon this metaphor of a farmer cultivating his field to interpret their own vocations. God had called them to ministries of encouragement or building up others in love. Like Paul and Jeremiah, coaches cannot make clients grow. Coaching finds its origins in God's desire to plant, cultivate, and build up a fruitful people. It involves cultivating the conditions where people can focus on who they are and where God wants them to go or grow. Coaching involves building up another through a ministry of encouragement, support, and challenge. Coaching is about cultivating people's courage to claim God's powerful intentions for their lives and to formulate these intentions into concrete life projects.

The real constraints or barriers in people's lives are not usually at the level of resources or abilities. They reside at the level of intention and imagination. Because the real barriers operate at this level, the energy for growth and transformation is within the client and not the coach. The coach can only cultivate or build up the conditions where these mental or behavioral logjams are removed sufficiently for the client to deepen his or her self-understanding and take meaningful, faithful action. The coach walks alongside the client, encouraging the conditions where growth occurs. The coach is not an expert who magically changes a client's life. No amount of advice, suggestion, or information can do that. The power for change comes from within the client, not the coach. The coach's task is one of cultivation and encouragement.

Many people in our own time know what it feels like to be plucked up or uprooted. They lose track of who they are amid all the responsibilities and enticements of daily life. They drift off-center, lacking a firm taproot to ground and nourish their souls. The soil of their lives grows dry, compacted, and hard. The weeds of other people's agendas and expectations grow up in their gardens, sapping them of their best energy and insight. When this happens, people cannot bear God's good fruit.

Coaches cultivate the conditions for encouragement and renewal in people's lives so seeds of loving, knowing, and serving God can sprout, blossom, and bear good fruit. Such cultivation, encouragement, and edification cannot make growth happen. But coaches can encourage and support people as they address the barriers that prevent them from finding and fulfilling their true vocation in God.

Coach as Tutor

Paul uses a second image that sheds light on coaching as a biblical practice. He twice makes reference to Christians needing a guardian or tutor as they grow in Christ: "For though you might have ten thousand guardians in Christ," he tells the Corinthians, "you do not have many fathers." (1 Cor 4:15) Again, in Galatians 4:24, he writes: "Therefore the law was our disciplinarian until Christ came." In both passages, the NRSV translates the Greek word *paidagogos* as either "guardian" or "disciplinarian." Yet neither translation captures accurately the specific meaning of the Greek word *paidagogos*.

Children in Greek households were usually under the care of a *paidagogos* from the ages of seven to eighteen. The *paidagogos* was not a teacher. He did not instruct children. Rather, he walked alongside them wherever they went (Bromley 1985, 753ff). The *paidagogos* accompanied children to school and saw they arrived safely. His goal was not intellectual understanding. It was the shaping of a virtuous life. The *paidagogos* gave practical guidance and direction. Paul is suggesting that Christians need someone to walk alongside them, to cultivate the conditions of encouragement and insight. This person is a partner, not a master, overseer, or teacher. The *paidagogos* offers encouragement, not instruction; guidance, not advice. Such a relationship helps us cultivate a virtuous life in Christ.

Coaching possesses many similarities to the ancient Greek *paidagogos*. In the same way as a *paidagogos* walked alongside a young Greek boy, a coach walks alongside someone to provide practical support and guidance. The coach's goal is not intellectual understanding but the shaping of a purposeful life. Both allow others to possess their own experience.

Both the coach and the *paidagogos* are genuinely committed to the well-being of the person alongside whom they walk. Without this basic commitment to the other person, a coach possesses only a bundle of tricks and techniques. Just as Greek children outgrew their *paidagogos* once they matured, so coaching's goal is for the client to become more independent and self-directed. Good coaches create conditions where they are no longer needed.

When my children were learning to ride a bicycle, my task was to run alongside them and steady them. They were engaged in learning a complex set of maneuvers all at once: steering, balancing, and coordinating hands and feet. As I jogged alongside them, I spoke encouraging words and reminded them of what they had already learned. I asked them to pay attention to what was happening in their bodies as they tried simultaneously to balance, steer, and move forward. I was always cheering and applauding their efforts, even when they fell off and skinned their knees. They eventually learned to ride their bicycles. What first seemed an impossible task now became second nature. They no longer needed me to steady, encourage, and remind them.

The *paidagogos* and the coach are a lot like this. When people are growing and changing, they benefit from a coach who walks alongside them. Sometimes this person just steadies them and speaks words of encouragement. Occasionally they will cry with them when they fall down and skin their knees. At other times, coaches challenge clients to pay attention so they can learn from their own experience. Amid the stress and anxiety of learning new behaviors, coaches remind clients what they already know and want to do. Coaches help clients balance, steer, and move forward all at once. And, once clients have learned to ride, coaches clap and cheer their performance. They have done the best job possible when their clients no longer need their assistance

Equipping the Saints for Ministry

The New Testament provides yet another helpful image for understanding how we live out our baptismal commitment to coach and be coached. Paul's letter to the Ephesians links the language of building up or edification with that of equipping. "The gifts he gave were that some would be apostles, some prophets, some evangelists, some pastors and teachers, to equip the saints for the work of ministry, for building up the body of Christ." (Eph 4:11-12)

The process of edification and up-building exists to equip Christians for the work of ministry. Coaching is not merely about individual learning and performance. It occurs for the sake of the larger community. The ministry of coaching adds value to both individual and organizational performance. ". . . [W]e must grow up in every way into him who is the head, into Christ, from whom the whole body, joined and knit together by every ligament with which it is equipped, as each part is working properly, promotes the body's growth in building itself up in love." (Eph 4:1, 15-16)

The key word is "equipping." Coaches do not mollify, cater, entertain, advise, or fix the saints. They equip the saints. They cultivate a climate of encouragement where people are built up for the work of ministry. Coaches increase people's awareness and accountability as they enter into ministries of service and witness for the sake of the church's participation in God's mission to the world. They encourage Christians to link their inner purposes and values to concrete daily circumstances, decisions, and choices so God's mission to the world is carried forward.

Barnabas and Ministries of Encouragement

Barnabas provides the clearest New Testament example of a ministry of encouragement, support, and challenge. Only Paul and Peter are mentioned more often than Barnabas in the book of Acts. Yet people often do not recognize his name. Barnabas frequently plays the role of a good coach who walks alongside others in order to equip, support, and hold them accountable for their ministries. One sees in Barnabas' ministry how *allelon* and *oikodomein* function to equip the saints for the work of ministry.

Barnabas' given name was Joseph. He was a Levite from Cyprus who encouraged the apostles' early ministry by selling his property for the benefit of their mission (Acts 4:36). When Saul (or Paul) came to Jerusalem after his conversion, most Christians wanted nothing to do with him. They knew him only as a persecutor and enemy of the church. This was the man who had orchestrated the stoning of Stephen. But Barnabas encouraged Paul to tell his story to the Jerusalem church; and he encouraged the Jerusalem elders to give Paul a second chance. "Barnabas took him, brought him to the apostles, and described for them how on the road he had seen the Lord, who had spoken to him, and how in Damascus he had spoken boldly in the name of Jesus." (Acts 9:27)

When the Gentile mission met with success in Antioch and the first Christian community was formed there, Barnabas went to encourage their work and support their mission. He immediately saw the possibilities for Paul and, going to Tarsus, he called Paul forth to support the work of the Antioch congregation. (Acts 11:22-26)

Barnabas later walked alongside Paul in his first missionary journey through Cyprus and Asia Minor. When the church at Antioch sent Paul to defend the Gentile mission before the Jerusalem Council, Barnabas again accompanied Paul.

Barnabas' ministry of encouragement and support extended beyond Paul. It included John Mark, Silas, and others. On their first missionary journey, John Mark had left their company in an act that Paul considered desertion. When Paul was about to embark on his second journey, Barnabas encouraged him to take John Mark. But Paul refused. So Barnabas and John Mark set off on one journey, while Paul took Silas and went on another. Apparently John Mark responded well to the trust given him by the "son of encouragement, "since we find that Paul later speaks of him as a valuable assistant." (2 Tim 4:11, Col 4:10, Phlm 24)

One can see many of the characteristics of effective Christian coaching in Barnabas' ministry of encouragement. When Paul had retired to Tarsus after his first visit to Jerusalem, Barnabas visited him and called him forth to ministry. It was Barnabas who encouraged Paul to hear God's call to ministry at Antioch. He invited the Jerusalem church into a new awareness of where God's Spirit was moving among the gentile mission and thus enabled them to take responsibility for new initiatives in mission. He walked alongside Paul as he took his first journeys as a Christian missionary. The book of Acts speaks of Barnabas as a partner in mission. He knew how to co-create partnerships in the gospel between individuals such as Paul and Mark as well as between communities at Jerusalem and Antioch. Barnabas' ministry added value both to the individuals whose lives he touched and to the early Christian movement as a whole.

Conclusion

While the Bible may never use the words *coach* or *coaching*, the lives of prophets and apostles frequently exemplify coaching as a style of relating to others. This relational style is marked by consistent, positive encouragement; dialogue and inquiry; constructive reflection; and a non-hierarchical relationship. It combines straightforwardness with kindness, attentive listening with forthright communication. It seeks to build one another up so that the saints are equipped for ministry.

Coaching as a Christian practice finds its deepest affirmation in the improbable belief that God chooses to act through people. Like Barnabas, coaches are encouragers who build up or cultivate others' gifts for ministry so they can become who God has already called them to be.

CHAPTER FOUR

Good Boundaries Make Good Neighbors: Coaching and Helping Relationships

Coaching can look like a number of other relationships, including counseling, consulting, mentoring, or even spiritual direction. It shares the same name as still another field of practice: athletic coaching or training. All these relationships attempt to move people from one place to another in their lives. They all rely on conversation and dialogue. All depend on establishing trust and safety. Several share overlapping theoretical foundations and common resources.

People consequently confuse these relationships with each other. Church leaders or Christian educators will call someone a coach in one breath and a mentor in the next, thus leaving the impression that both terms are merely two ways of describing the same thing. This lack of clarity makes it critically important to establish boundaries between these unique fields of practice.

No one would mow their lawn with a chainsaw. Nor would someone change a flat tire with a vacuum cleaner. The inability to differentiate between coaching and these other disciplines can lead to the equivalent of mowing the lawn with a chainsaw. To get the results we want, we must choose a tool appropriate for the task. Coaching is one more resource in the church leader's toolkit. But it is only effective when used under the proper conditions.

Numerous pitfalls face coaching so long as people are unsure where coaching leaves off and counseling, consulting, or mentoring begin. First, coaching will have difficulty emerging as a distinctive practice available to Christian educators and church leaders so long as they cannot distinguish it from other helping relationships. Second, coaching will continue to suffer from the stigma of being regarded as the same thing counselors or consultants have always done but now rebaptized with a new name. Third, people with critical mental health needs may find themselves in coaching relationships from which they will not benefit

Finally, coaches may feel misunderstood and misused by congregations or church leaders who relate to them as consultants rather than as coaches. Christian educators or church leaders who come to coaching without a clear picture of what coaches actually do will bring expectations shaped by their previous experiences with consultants. These mismatched expectations can lead to frustration, confusion, or disappointment. As a result, former clients may promote the impression that coaching is not really effective and most coaches are poorly equipped for what they do.

What, then, distinguishes coaching from these other, related fields of practice?

Coaching and Athletic Training

Athletic training is perhaps the easiest discipline to distinguish from coaching. The general public has traditionally associated *coach* and *coaching* with athletic training. As early as the nineteenth century, coaching was used to describe the training, motivation, and guidance of athletes for their best performance. Many sports metaphors continue to permeate both professional and life coaching.

Coaching for ministry and athletic training do share some similarities. Athletic coaching implies motivation, learning, accountability, and a desire for the best performance possible. Athletic coaching fosters a strong interpersonal relationship between the player and the coach. Coaching for ministry similarly relies on a strong interpersonal alliance between coach and client. It also uses accountability and the tapping of inner motivation to help people achieve more and learn faster.

On the other hand, a ministry coach is distinctly different from an athletic coach. Athletic coaches always remain in a superior position to their players. Coaches are the experts; players, the learners. Most athletic coaches establish learning objectives and performance goals for their players. These objectives are typically mastered in a linear way. Players first learn a basic routine; they then learn how to embellish or elaborate on it. The coach sets the sequence and scope of these learning objectives and monitors performance to control the players' progression toward competency. A coach's superior expertise makes him or her qualified to establish learning objectives and assess progress toward them.

Most athletic coaches also try to identify wrong behaviors and correct them. The golf coach watches how players hold their clubs and then corrects the hand positioning to improve performance, for instance. A high school coach watches how basketball players stand incorrectly in shooting freethrows. The coach then directly instructs them on how to stand and shoot.

Coaching for ministry diverges greatly from these aspects of athletic coaching. Ministry coaches are not experts. They are instead partners and co-creators of designed alliances with their clients. Ministry coaches do not determine the sequence and scope of what clients will learn. By and large, progression is not linear and straightforward. Most coaching clients go through cycles of progress and regression. Learning is sometimes iterative rather than linear. Furthermore, a coaching client always sets the agenda and maintains control over the direction and pace of the relationship. Nor do ministry coaches focus on correcting errors. The ministry coach's goal is future-oriented learning and performance, not correction of previous errors based on some template of "good" and "bad" behavior.

Coaching and Counseling

Differences between coaching and athletic training are relatively simple to identify. To differentiate between coaching and counseling presents a more difficult challenge.

Superficial similarities can lull observers into believing they are identical practices. Both disciplines use many of the same tools and strategies. Coaches and therapists listen closely, empathize, ask good questions, and challenge assumptions. Both are skilled in such practices as reframing, establishing trust, and building rapport. They both assist clients in goal setting and decision making. How then does one distinguish between coaching and counseling or therapy?

Shared Theoretical Roots of Counseling and Coaching

Unfortunately, the line between coaching and counseling is not always clear. This blurred boundary partially derives from their common roots. Coaching and counseling both draw their theoretical underpinnings from the work of psychologists such as Alfred Adler, Carl Jung, Abraham Maslow, and Milton Erikson. Coaching's emphasis on vision and values, for instance, draws heavily on Adler's belief that people develop a unique life approach, which shapes their goals, habits, and values. It also echoes Jung's emphasis on living one's life purposefully. His theleological belief that we invent our futures through our visions has also influenced coaching emphasis on vision and the future. Humanistic psychology also figures prominently in both the coaching and counseling literature, especially Maslow's language of self-actualization. Other aspects of coaching depend on Milton Erikson's psychological insights into how language and powerful questions can trigger transformational change.

With such similar roots, what really distinguishes coaching as a separate discipline? Indeed, critics worry that some coaches may actually be doing harm to people who are receiving coaching but actually need psychotherapy. These same critics complain that coaching may provide a convenient excuse for people who need therapeutic intervention but are avoiding it by talking to a coach.

While there is considerable overlap between counseling and coaching skills, both the International Coach Federation (ICF) and individual coaches make a vigorous distinction between coaching and counseling (ICF 2005; Grodzki 2002:10-21; Williams & Davis 2002:40-41). Coaching and counseling work with different populations, have differing goals, possess divergent orientations toward time, and have distinctive ways of structuring the client relationship. (See Figure 4.1)

Different Goals in Coaching and Counseling

Therapists and counselors have traditionally worked with people who bear a burden of emotional pain rooted in their past experiences. This emotional pain has impaired their effective functioning. Through the healing of this past pain, they

Figure 4.1 A Comparison of Coaching and Counseling

Category	Coaching	Counseling
Population Served	Basically Healthy People Wanting To Accomplish More	People in Emotional Pain
Time Perspective	Future	Past
Goal of Relationship	Create the Future	Fix or Heal the Past
Pace	Faster, Immediate Time Frame	Slower, Long-Term
Focus	Real World Results	Inner World Interpretations
Setting	Flexible Times and Settings	Private, Consistent Time & Space
Relationship	Mutuality & Partnership	Hierarchical, Counselor is Expert

can be restored to more effective living. Counseling thus emphasizes healing and the processing of emotion. The counselor's goal is to heal past emotional pain so clients are more able to cope with their present lives and relationships.

Coaching, on the other hand, is oriented toward learning and performance. Coaching is for people who are basically healthy but want to accomplish more. Coaches are more focused on wellness than on pathology. They see their clients as healthy and whole rather than broken and limited. Unlike most therapy, coaching has no "identified patient." There are only people who are trying their best but have become bogged down or stuck and who need an opportunity to re-orient and renew their lives.

Different Orientations Toward Time

Counseling orients itself primarily toward the past, where the client's emotional pain first emerged as a problem. Therapists encourage clients to look back into their personal histories to find healing for present pain or dysfunction. The goal is to resolve past trauma so they can function more adequately in their present lives. Counseling thus focuses on the client's previous emotional and psychological history.

Coaching takes church leaders or Christian educators who are functioning reasonably well and helps them grow toward higher levels of performance and learning. The focus is on the future, not the past. Coaches support clients as they clarify vision, identify barriers, set goals, plan, and engage in reflection-in-action. They help clients explore the kind of future they want to create. They encourage people to live purposefully and to act in ways consistent with their deepest values. Whereas a coach would ask *how* a client can move forward, a counselor seeks to find answers in the client's past history for *why* they act as they do now.

Different Orientations Toward Inner and Outer Worlds

Therapists are more apt to focus on process, feelings, and the client's inner world. As a result, therapists are free to move at a slower pace and to examine reflectively the client's inner world. Coaches, conversely, are more oriented to outcomes, actions, and the client's outer life. The client's inner world has importance only insofar as the client needs to link inner values to concrete actions. Coaches thus move at a faster pace so clients can produce concrete results in areas where they want to see progress. While counseling frames progress as a slow and often painful process, coaching assumes that growth can be rapid and even enjoyable.

Different Settings

The two disciplines also have different settings. Counseling usually occurs in controlled, consistent, and private settings. The counseling conversation has a fixed time and happens at regularly scheduled intervals. Sessions almost always occur face-to-face. Coaching, on the other hand, is much more flexible. Some coaches meet clients in face-to-face settings. Others use the telephone for appointments with clients. The coaching schedule itself may be fluid and dynamic. Rather than talk on the phone or meet in the coach's office, they may hold a session at the client's workplace.

How Power and Responsibility Function in the Relationship

Coaches and therapists also handle power differently. Most therapists operate from a medical model. The therapist is the expert; the client, the patient. Clients come with problems they expect the "expert" to "fix." The therapist functions as a professional who possesses special expertise. The counselor uses his or her professional expertise to guide people along a pathway that leads toward more effective functioning.

While therapy is usually a hierarchical relationship based on the power of expertise, coaching is always a collaborative partnership between equals. Coach and client are co-active in designing their alliance. Clients remain the experts on their own work and experience. They retain the power to define themselves and their situations.

There are three principles behind all coaching:

1. The client has responsibility for defining the relationship.
2. The client has responsibility for deciding what to do.
3. The client has responsibility for the outcomes of actions he or she takes.

The coach never takes responsibility away from the client. Whereas the counselor is responsible professionally for both process and outcome, the coach takes responsibility only for process and never for a client's decisions, actions, or outcomes.

Because of the therapeutic function of transference and counter-transference in the counseling relationship, therapists usually behave in indirect ways. They may even take on the qualities of a nurturing parent. This strategy requires limited self-disclosure by the therapist. If a therapist and client met in the grocery store, they certainly would not speak; and they might not even acknowledge one another.

Coaches, on the other hand, are typically more direct and straightforward.

Because typical therapeutic principles like transference and counter-transference are not part of the coaching process, coaches are more apt to engage in appropriate self-disclosure. They are more likely to see such self-disclosure as occasionally useful as an aid to learning. Coaches will probably speak to clients or even have social interactions with them outside the coaching relationship.

While boundaries are more permeable between coaches and clients than between counselors and their clients, both coaches and therapists maintain strict boundaries regarding physical or sexual relationships. It is never appropriate for romantic or sexual relationships to develop between a coach and client. Some denominations have guidelines and policies regarding such professional relationships. All are grounded in Paul's advice to Timothy: "Do not speak harshly to an older man, but speak to him as to a father, to younger men as brothers, to older women as mothers, to younger women as sisters—with absolute purity." (1 Tim 5:1-2)

Similar Techniques but Different Purposes and Contexts

These distinctions explain how counseling and coaching may use many of the same methods, but toward different ends and within different relational contexts. Both counseling and coaching, for example, ask questions, listen carefully, establish rapport or trust, make suggestions, or propose assignments. Both use language as the primary tool for change and transformation. But these specific skills are directed toward different goals.

While a therapist may listen for symptoms or problems, a coach listens primarily for values and ego strength. A counselor might listen without any particular solution in mind. A coach, on the other hand, may be listening for underlying assumptive patterns that get in the way of achievement. A counselor might interpret strong emotions as an indication that something is wrong. Coaches assume emotions are a normal and natural part of human experience.

These distinctions are somewhat overdrawn, as all attempts to model or categorize whole professions always are. They do, however, suggest that coaching and counseling are two ends of a single continuum. At many points between these two poles, they overlap and their boundaries blur—particularly where both professions draw on some of the same tools and strategies.

Coaches Need to be Prepared to Refer Clients to a Therapist

One important skill that coaches must possess, even if they do not have a counseling background, is the ability to recognize and value the difference between coaching and therapy. They also must have the capacity to recognize when a client may need counseling rather than coaching.

There are at least ten indicators that someone may need a mental health professional rather than a coach. (Meinke, 2005) Coaches need to recognize these indicators and be prepared to refer clients to qualified mental health professionals. These warning signs include:

1. Increased expressions of hopelessness or helplessness
2. The inability to focus because of intrusive thoughts
3. Ongoing poor sleep patterns that lead to excessive tiredness
4. A sudden, marked change in appetite
5. Strong or persistent expressions of guilt, shame, or unworthiness
6. Expressions of despair or hopelessness
7. Feeling constantly over-tired or hyper-energized
8. Hyper-irritability or sudden and unpredictable outbursts of anger
9. Impulsive behavior with no thoughts about consequences or risks
10. Preoccupation with thoughts about one's own death or the death of others

This list is by no means comprehensive. Coaches should pay attention to other behaviors or expressions, such as excessive or ongoing grief. Hints of or actual evidence of substance abuse and addictions are another indication that a client may need therapy rather than coaching. Coaches themselves should not attempt to address these issues. Addictions, thoughts of suicide, clinical depression, or other behaviors should be handled by qualified mental health professionals and not by coaches.

Given these warning signals for referral, novice coaches might be tempted to interpret any emotional behavior as sufficient cause to terminate coaching and refer to a therapist. Just because someone becomes emotional does not mean they are dysfunctional, however. Feelings themselves are not a sign of dysfunction or mental illness. Expressing emotions can actually be very healthy if shared in appropriate times and ways. The coach's task is to assess whether such emotional expressions are appropriate or not. Does a client's moodiness or tearfulness continue inappropriately? Do they seem to interfere with the client's thinking, work, or other relationships?

Determining whether people need coaching or therapy depends upon the degree to which they have become unable to move forward on their own. Someone needing a mental health professional cannot go further without significant help. Someone needing a coach may feel stuck, confused, or bogged down; but with some support they can move ahead.

Our farm is located a few miles outside town. Particularly in the early spring, teenagers drive into our pasture believing they have found a good place for a secluded party. Unknowingly, they drive into a water-logged field and their cars sink up to their axles in mud. When this happens, we take our tractor or pick-up truck and pull them out. Once freed from the mud, they go on their way. They possess skill enough to know what they are doing and their car still moves on its own power.

Not far from these same fields is an old railroad crossing. It is poorly maintained and very rough. If you go over it too fast, you can easily tear off your muffler. A few years ago, some teenagers went racing down our road. The car's sixteen-year-old driver was trying to impress his female passengers. Driving far too carelessly, he lost control of the car when it hit the rough crossing. It flew into the air, turned over in the cornfield, and began to catch on fire. Had my neighbor not heard the crash and rushed down to pull everyone from the smoldering car, some of the passengers would have lost their lives.

This was something quite different than a few teenagers pulling into the pasture for a party and getting stuck in the mud. A crumpled, burned-out vehicle was not going anywhere on its own. Neither were its passengers. Some had broken legs and arms. One had a concussion. What led to this accident was not just a lack of understanding about rural fields after spring rains. It was reckless and self-destructive behavior.

People who benefit from coaching are like cars driven into our pasture. They get stuck in the mud; but, with a little help, they can get moving again. People who need a mental health professional are more like the car that crashed into our neighbor's cornfield. The vehicle and its passengers were not going any farther on their own. They needed significant outside assistance just to survive.

If coaches feel a client needs the help of a mental health professional, then they should be prepared to address this issue with the client. The coach can give feedback on what he or she observes. Together the client and coach can pursue the possible need for outside therapy. In some cases, coaches may need to terminate their coaching alliance to make clear to a client that his or her issues are not appropriate for a coaching relationship.

Many coaches have a working relationship with counselors or therapists in their area. Counselors often appreciate a working relationship with coaches to whom they can refer clients. Given their existing caseloads and the constraints of third-party insurance regulations, they may be happy to refer people who really do not need therapy but who could benefit from coaching. Conversely, most coaches eventually encounter clients who need therapy, not coaching. In these cases, it is helpful for coaches to have a prior working relationship with several counselors to whom they can make referrals.

In some cases, clients may work simultaneously with a coach and a therapist. When this happens, the client should disclose he or she is working with a therapist. And the coach should insist the client share with his or her counselor about having a coach. In most cases, it is best for people to complete their therapeutic work before entering into a coaching relationship. Coaching can never be a substitute for psychotherapeutic work. Coaches should never collude with clients who are avoiding serious psychotherapeutic issues by talking to a coach instead of a mental health professional.

Coaching and Consulting

Consulting, like therapy, shares many common theoretical foundations and techniques with coaching. Coaching, like consulting, draws upon organizational development theory, blending it with personal development training and humanistic psychology. Because many consulting firms increasingly offer coaching as one of their services, the lines between coaching and consulting can easily blur. While coaching and consulting share some common background, significant differences separate them. (See Figure 4.2)

Coaches Do Not Come as Content Experts

Individuals or organizations typically retain a consultant if they need specialized expertise or knowledge. When an organization or individual hires a consultant, they usually want this consultant to have specific knowledge of the proposed subject area or industry. A business executive in the asphalt business, for example, might take early retirement and work as a self-employed consultant to asphalt companies. But he is likely neither to seek nor to obtain contracts with bioengineering corporations.

Coaches, on the other hand, rarely function as content experts. They do not necessarily possess previous experience in or specific knowledge of a client's own career, occupation, or life situation. In fact, some coaches believe it is better not to share their clients' subject matter expertise or work experience. If coaches know something about their clients' businesses, they may drift inadvertently into giving advice based on their own knowledge or experience. If clients know their coaches have expertise in their field or occupation, they may unconsciously begin looking to them for advice or treat them as consultants with expertise superior to their own.

If I have been successful in redeveloping congregations in transition, for example, I may have certain assumptions about what redevelopment "ought" to

Figure 4.2 Comparison of Coaching and Consulting

Category	Coaching	Consulting
Expertise	Expertise in process but not content	Specialized knowledge of content area or industry required
Relationship	Symmetrical partnership	Asymmetrical, hierarchical with consultant expected to have special expertise
Scope	Wide scope that may include both professional and personal	Narrow scope limited to specific topic, problem, or challenge
Process	Stands with client and helps to identify challenge, then walks with client for support, challenge, and accountability	Gathers information, diagnoses, prescribes, recommends
Nature of client	Usually an individual, occasionally a team or group	May be an individual, team, department, division, or even a whole organization

look like. When a client violates one of my unspoken assumptions about good redevelopment, I may be tempted to correct or advise her on what she should do. As a result, I am putting my agenda ahead of the client's. I make myself an obstacle to the client's own learning, goal-setting, and achievement. Coaches have process skills. They bring these process skills into the collaborative partnerships with clients. But it is always and only the client who is the expert on his life or work.

Coaches Do Not Diagnose, Prescribe, and Make Recommendations

While consulting approaches vary, most assume the consultant comes as an outside expert, gathers information, diagnoses problems, and prescribes recommended solutions. In some cases, the consultant may also guide the implementation of his or her recommendations.

Coaches, on the other hand, do not diagnose, design, or recommended solutions for their clients. Coaches walk alongside others helping them to discover, design, and implement their own answers. They are partners with their clients rather than experts superior to them. Coaches do not adopt a position of expertise and superior knowledge from which they advise or recommend particular solutions to their clients. While a consultant may produce a final report with recommendations and step-by-step plans, coaching never results in such a document.

Coaching Does Not Have a Predetermined, Fixed Scope

Consultants usually have a fixed scope to their work. They work within the parameters of the issue or challenge the employing organization or individual has defined for them. This gives a narrow focus to most consulting relationships.

Coaches, on the other hand, typically retain the freedom and flexibility to address a wider range of issues. While clients might come to coaching because of a particular issue or challenge, the actual coaching may cover a much broader field of professional and even personal issues. Coaches do not believe that people live their lives in separate compartments. The personal impacts the professional. Work influences personal life. Limiting the scope of the coaching to one narrow segment of life or work undermines its capacity to partner with the client for significant learning and performance improvement.

Coaches Do Not Work With Whole Organizations

A consultant may work with an individual, a team, a department, a division, or even a whole organization. Consulting clients come in a variety of sizes and organizational shapes. Coaching, on the other hand, is usually a one-to-one relationship. In a few cases, a coach may work with a team to improve its learning and performance. Seldom does a coach work with a whole organization, however. Even when an organization contracts with a coach, it is typically to work with individual executives or employees.

Two Points On a Continuum

Like any model or descriptive comparison, this discussion somewhat exaggerates the characteristics of both coaching and consulting. There are always some coaches that specialize in clients with backgrounds or occupations similar to their own. Some consultants adopt a more collaborative and open-ended approach. They see their role as helping the organization learn to diagnose and respond to its own challenges rather than providing expert advice in a final report. As with psychotherapy, it may be best to consider coaching and consulting as two poles along a continuum. The further one moves toward the extremes of this continuum, the sharper the differences between these two professions. As one moves toward the middle, however, they begin to blur.

Maintaining a clear boundary between coaching and consulting allows both fields of practice to carry out their work with the least confusion and frustration. The individual or organization needs to be clear at all times whether they are interacting with someone as a coach or as a consultant. This clarity helps the individual or organization avoid conflating these two distinct practices, expecting the coach to consult or the consultant to coach.

Introducing Coaching Means Re-educating Congregations and Leaders

Not long ago, a regional church body introduced coaching as a tool for church re-development in its judicatory. Judicatory leaders trained coaches to work with congregational teams in designing and implementing church transformation projects. The project coordinator soon began receiving complaints from both the coaches and congregations.

When these complaints were further explored, it became evident that the coaches were acting in ways consistent with their training. The congregations, however, had become so accustomed to consultancy relationships with regional staff that they could not make the switch to a coaching relationship. They expected the coaches to behave as had their many previous consultants. They wanted these newly-minted coaches to function as experts who came into the congregation, gathered information, diagnosed what it should do, and prepared a prescriptive report with recommendations.

Most congregations had been through this consulting cycle many times. It had almost never resulted in significant transformation, which was why they were still on a redevelopment list. It also explained why the denomination was attempting to move out of its old consultancy model and try something different. Once the consultant delivered his or her report, the congregation put it on a shelf and ignored it. What did some outside expert know about their congregation and community? The consultant's parental, one-up role gave the congregation permission to behave like any rebellious child.

But now, when their newly assigned coaches refused to act like consultants, the congregations were confused. In some cases, the reaction turned from confusion to anger and accusation. The congregational teams felt their coaches were somehow poorly trained or incompetent. They were not performing as the consultants with whom they had previously worked.

Over several decades, most church governing bodies and judicatories have conditioned congregations to expect consulting services from denominational offices. Church judicatories often promoted this expectation. As older missional justifications for judicatory staff and resources waned, most congregations continued to support a strong judicatory role for consulting services. So, when a regional denominational body tentatively introduced coaching, one would naturally expect them to resist these efforts.

If middle governing bodies or denominations are to shift from consulting to coaching, they will need to engage in significant interpretive work with congregations and church leaders. They must focus on both sides of the equation: congregational leaders and coaches. It is not enough simply to train coaches who can work with church planters, redevelopers, Christian educators, or other congregational leaders. Coaches can be adequately prepared and well-trained. But if congregations and their leaders have not recalibrated their expectations, everyone will experience frustration.

Judicatories have successfully trained congregations and church leaders to expect consulting. Congregations have learned to avoid awareness of and responsibility for their own transformation. To change this dynamic will take intentional work by both congregations and denominational staff. Both parties will have to invest time, thought, and energy into understanding the distinctions between coaching and consulting. Both will have significant relearning to do if coaching is to become a standard part of the denominational toolkit for transformation.

Otherwise most Christian educators will continue to treat their new coaches as subject matter experts in educational methods and learning. Most church planters and redevelopers will relate to their coaches as consultants on organizational, evangelistic, and outreach programs. No matter how hard coaches try to function as partners in discovery and learning, they will find their clients forcing them back into old consulting patterns. They will force coaches into the well-worn mold of consultants with their specialized expertise, techniques, and knowledge.

Coaching and Mentoring

Mentoring is often confused with coaching. Many people use the words *coaching* and *mentoring* interchangeably. While both mentoring and coaching share many of the same skills and techniques, they are distinctly different practices. (See Figure 4.3)

The term *mentor* derives from Homer's Greek epic about Odysseus and the Trojan War. When Odysseus leaves for Troy, he places his son, Telemachus, in the care of his friend, Mentor. A mentor, consequently, has traditionally been an individual—usually older and always more experienced—who helps and guides another person's development. This younger, less experienced person is sometimes called a protégé or mentee.

Figure 4.3   Comparison of Coaching and Mentoring

Category	Coaching	Mentoring
Relationship	Exists to benefit client	Mutual benefit for mentor and protege
Scope	All of client's personal and professional life	Socialization into profession or organization
Expertise	Mutual Partner	Possesses Greater Experience or Skills
Impact	Client responsible for own success. Coach supports, cheerleads, holds accountable	Includes career sponsorship and direct advocacy

Characteristics of a Good Mentor

A mentor therefore is someone who (a) has experienced the challenges a novice now faces; (b) possesses the ability to communicate his or her experience; and (c) is willing to do so. A mentor takes a special interest in helping a less experienced novice develop into a successful professional. Mentors usually are advocates for their protégés' career development and advancement. They can open doors for protégés, introducing them to individuals or networks that will advance their careers.

Mentoring is common in business settings, where newly hired or newly promoted employees are given a formal mentor. A mentor's task is to help the protégé learn organizational policies, procedures, and culture. Mentors may also help recently promoted executives master the skills and expectations of their new roles.

Mentoring is also very common in educational settings. Schools often assign mentors to help newly minted teachers make the transition from being full-time students to being classroom educators. Similarly, a graduate student's dissertation advisor or research director serves as an informal mentor. Advisors socialize students into their chosen profession's ethics and ethos. They introduce their younger colleagues to networks that promote job advancement or research opportunities.

A whole range of social service agencies also rely on mentoring. At-risk children and youth, for example, may be assigned a mentor. The fundamental mission of an agency such as Big Brothers/Big Sisters is to provide children and youth with mentors during critical transitional years.

Traditional mentoring was often informal. A more experienced church leader or Christian educator would befriend and nurture someone with less experience. The relationship was typically unstructured and clearly asymmetrical.

More experienced leaders were often drawn to mentoring because they saw it as benefiting them as well as their protégés. Both people received ego satisfaction from the relationship. The mentor got the satisfaction of seeing someone else grow through their nurturing and support. The protégé gained a feeling of being valued by someone they admired and respected.

Coaching Compared to Mentoring

Coaching differs in several respects from mentoring. While the mentor's primary responsibility is to socialize someone into a new profession or organizational responsibility, coaches do not limit themselves to such a narrow focus. Coaching entails much more than socialization into an organization or orientation into new job responsibilities. Coaches are apt to see the whole of a client's personal and professional life as appropriate for coaching conversations.

Mentors often see themselves as passing on their hard-won insights, knowledge, and expertise to a new generation. They define themselves as more skilled and knowledgeable than the protégés they mentor. Coaches, on the other hand, walk alongside others as equal partners and collaborators.

Mentors often open professional doors for their protégés and directly assist them in career advancement through personal introductions and sponsorship. Coaches are equally committed to their clients' advancement and achievement. Yet they do not directly sponsor their client's advancement.

Perhaps the most important distinction between mentors and coaches lies in what each expects to receive back from those with whom they work. Mentors and protégés both expect to receive ego satisfaction from their relationship. Both contribute to the relationship and expect to receive back from it. The mentor receives back affirmation and appreciation from someone younger. Protégés can serve as stimuli for regeneration and renewal when a well-established professional has plateaued in his or her work. The protégé's energy and new ways of thinking expand the mentor's own professional horizons.

The coaching relationship, on the other hand, exists solely for the client's benefit. Both the client and the coach contribute equally to this relationship; but they are not equal partners in receiving its benefits. The coaching relationship is collaboratively co-created by coach and client; and it is completely focused on the client and his or her needs. The client grants power not to the coach but to the relationship. This is distinctly different from the mentor-protégé relationship, which is much more rooted in the personal relationship between mentor and protégé.

Since the client is granting power to the relationship and not to the coach, the client never gives away his or her own power. Because clients retain all their own power, they also retain full responsibility for their actions and the consequences flowing from them.

This locus of power within the coaching relationship lies at the heart of its distinctiveness not only from mentoring but also from consulting and counseling. The power contributed by both coach and client to the relationship makes the relationship itself a power source upon which the client can depend. This important distinction keeps coaching from drifting into the asymmetrical power dynamics not only of mentoring but also of consulting and counseling.

Coaching and Spiritual Direction

Spiritual direction or spiritual guidance is an ancient ministry of the Christian church. The church's geographic and theological diversity mean that different Christian traditions give different meanings to spiritual direction. In addition to this basic diversity among different Christian traditions, there are both formal and informal models of spiritual direction across many traditions. Informal approaches may be as simple as two friends meeting for mutual support. More formal spiritual direction involves an intentionally structured relationship between a director with specialized training and a directee.

What is Spiritual Direction?

Perhaps the oldest and most widely quoted definition of spiritual direction comes from William Barry and William Connolly's *The Practice of Spiritual Direction* (1982). According to Barry and Connolly, spiritual direction helps people focus on what happens when they listen and respond to the God who is always communicating with humankind. Spiritual direction concerns itself with the person's concrete experiences of God. The directee is not helped to understand this relationship better or to theorize about it but actually to engage in it.

Spiritual directors help people pay attention to God's self-giving communication to them. They also guide the directee in responding to God, growing in intimacy with God, and living out the fruit of this divine-human relationship in daily life. The purpose of Christian spiritual direction is not ideas, concepts, or beliefs. It is experience.

Our experience of God's self-communicating love is not an isolated or rare experience but an ongoing and continual one. We are always in the presence of God; it is not something we manipulate or manage to make appear and disappear. What is lacking is an awareness of God's nearness. Christian spiritual direction helps people attend to this ever-present, ongoing experience of God's self-communication to them.

According to Barry and Connelly, Christian spiritual direction is the core from which all other forms of pastoral care and counseling flow. All other practices of Christian ministry radiate outward from the basic goal of helping people center their lives in the Mystery we name God.

Comparing and Contrasting Spiritual Direction to Coaching

This definition clarifies the boundaries between Christian spiritual direction and coaching for ministry. (See Figure 4.4) Spiritual direction's goal is to help people listen and respond to the God who speaks through their experiences, grow in intimacy with this God and live out the consequences of this intimacy in daily life. Spiritual direction helps people clarify and discern their religious experiences. Coaching's goals, on the other hand, are learning and performance. Coaching helps people clarify their values and purposes so they can take significant action toward specific changes they want to make. It is action-oriented.

Spiritual direction may include direct teaching of specific methods of prayer. While coaching includes some teaching and instruction about coaching tools and language, it generally does not include direct instruction of the client.

Because spiritual direction's goal is deepening the directee's relationship with God, this divine-human relationship is the focus of spiritual direction. The key relationship is not between the director and the directee but between the directee and God. In this sense, spiritual direction resembles coaching. Both coaching and spiritual direction do not intentionally seek to foster the experience of transference often essential to therapeutic healing.

Without transference as a goal, both coaches and spiritual directors may be more direct and unambiguous with their clients or directees than a counselor or therapist would be. Coaches and spiritual directors can be visible and very human companions on the same journey as their clients or directees. But coaching generally treats the coaching relationship itself as central to the coaching process. Coach and client work together to design an alliance that supports the client's goals and agenda.

The reasons people come to coaching also differ from why someone seeks out a spiritual director. People come to spiritual direction because they are searching for God. They want to understand their religious experiences or find the religious dimension of all their experiences. People seek out coaching because they feel stuck or bogged down and want to achieve more or learn faster in order to get the results they want from life.

In the end, spiritual directors do not seek to produce good church members or active apostles. Their goal is to foster a relationship of love and intimacy between God and their directees. Coaching's aim, on the other hand, is to foster conditions where people can take actions that help them achieve concrete goals they have established for themselves.

As with the previously mentioned helping relationships, nothing prevents coaches and spiritual directors from collaborating. After coaching a particular client for several sessions, a coach might realize that this particular client may benefit more from spiritual direction. The issue could be discussed with the client. Arrangements might even be made for the client to return to coaching after a period of spiritual direction. Alternatively, a coach and spiritual director might work concurrently with a client so long as all parties are clear about each other's boundaries and responsibilities.

Figure 4.4 Comparison of Coaching and Spiritual Direction

Category	Coaching	Spiritual Direction
Relationship	What happens as client and coach co-create alliance for learning and change is important	What happens between directee and God is important
Method	Very little direct teaching. Coach's responsibility is for process, not content.	Director may teach methods of prayer, give suggestions for retreats or meditation tools. Director is responsible for content and process.
Reason for Encounter	Seek to achieve more, learn faster	Searching for God, understand religious experience
Interpersonal Presence	No therapeutic role for transference so coach is visible as a person	No therapeutic role for transference so director is visible as companion on same spiritual journey

CHAPTER FIVE

A SEASON TO EVERYTHING: THE COACHING CONVERSATION'S RHYTHM AND FLOW

No definition can convey what actually happens in coaching. Coaches need more than definitions and descriptions. They need to have a good grasp of coaching's tools, processes, and strategies. One fundamental resource in every coach's toolkit is an understanding of the basic sequence of how coaches and clients work together from the beginning of their alliance until its completion. While every coaching alliance is unique, all share some common tasks and predictable stages. (See Figure 5.1) This chapter explores basic strategies for co-designing this alliance. It then describes the components of a coaching conversation.

Stages in the Coaching Alliance

The First Task: Cultivating Courageous Space

Coaches co-create a unique partnership with their clients. People come to coaching because they experience God calling them forth to larger purposes. They realize that responding to this call will not happen without courageous action on their part. Coaches can support, challenge, and encourage; but people must find within themselves the courage to trust God and take action. From the very beginning, coaches are co-creating an environment where people can act courageously.

Figure 5.1 Stages, Tasks, and Behaviors of the Coaching Process

STAGE	TASK	BEHAVIORS AND RESOURCES
1. Cultivating Courageous Space	Build Safety ————— Establish Trust	Nonjudgmental acceptance Confidentiality ————— Demonstrate Genuine Concern Coaching Competency Communication Share Control & Power
2. The Initial Session	Getting Acquainted ————— Establishing Primary Focus of Relationship ————— Formalizing an Agreement ————— Introduction to Basic Tools	Welcome Letter Personal Information Getting to Know You Worksheet ————— Primary Focus Worksheet ————— Signed, Written Agreement ————— Accountability Requesting Resistance & Sabotage Client is Responsible
3. Connecting Purpose to Action	Clarifying Vision, Values, or Purpose Focus on Action and Learning Confronting Self-Limiting Behaviors	Full Range of Coaching Practices

4.	Terminating	Naming Completion Behaviors
Coming to Closure		Revisit Original Primary Focus
		Reviewing Progress and Relationship
		Celebrating
		Negotiate Next Phase in Relationship
	Re-Negotiating	Establishing New Agreement
	Referring	Referral to Other Caches or Counselors

Cultivating this space continues throughout the coaching partnership. The process never ends; but it especially crucial in the very earliest interactions between coaches and clients. Two of its primary characteristics are safety and trust. From their very first encounter with a potential client, coaches are working to build these qualities into their alliance.

CREATING SAFE SPACE

Though it may sound paradoxical, courageous space must also be safe space. If people are going to take the risk of creating not just a life that works but a life that counts, they need at least one place in their lives that feels safe. They need a place where they can look honestly and truthfully at the lives they have already created. Safe space provides an environment where they feel free to try new things. Safe space allows people the freedom to discover the optimism and hope needed to respond to new possibilities.

Safety does not diminish the need for hard work. It does not make courage any less necessary. Safety in the coaching relationship has two components: nonjudgmental acceptance and confidentiality.

Nonjudgmental Acceptance. Safe environments are characterized by nonjudgmental acceptance. A climate of nonjudgmental acceptance allows people to speak the difficult truths that lead to transformation. When people fear they will be judged or criticized, they withhold part of the truth. Yet, until they can speak this truth, they cannot move forward.

When people do not feel they are in safe space, they become more concerned with looking good than with being real. As a result, they distort and limit their self-awareness. Most people only risk the vulnerability that leads to self-awareness when they feel they are in an accepting, nonjudgmental environment. Creating conditions that lead to self-awareness is crucial to the coaching alliance. Only when people are self-aware can they take responsibility for actions that change the conditions of their lives.

Nonjudgmental acceptance is as much felt as spoken. It is characterized by suspension of judgment and detachment.

Suspension of judgment involves stepping aside from making judgments about another person's life. When people judge, they make attributions of "good" or "bad." This stance has consequences for both the client and the coach. Once coaches move to a place of judgment, they cease to listen. Yet without accurate information, their perceptions grow increasingly distorted. At the same time, few clients are willing to speak truthfully and honestly about themselves when they are in the presence of judgment. They either become silent or censor their language, saying only what they believe acceptable to their hearers. The coaching partnership thus ceases to be a place of truthfulness and honesty.

We all know we are not to pass judgment. Unfortunately, the human brain seems hardwired for rushing to judgment. So what can coaches do to suspend judgment?

The best way to suspend judgment is to identify with the other person rather than to set oneself over against them. We recognize that we too have our own unique version of this same behavior. We acknowledge that the limitations and broken humanity we experience in another person are also within us. Observing human frailties in others, we take responsibility for ourselves rather than focusing on them. By this admission, we convert our judgment into solidarity and empathy.

The New Testament word for judgment, *krino*, literally means "to separate." (Bromley,1985, p. 469) When we judge, we separate ourselves from others. We act as if the flaws we see in them cannot possibly exist in us. Indeed, one way to deny our flaws and shortcomings is to project them onto someone else and then judge them as wanting. Focusing our judgment on another person, we do not have to examine ourselves.

Jesus' Sermon on the Mount beautifully describes this process: "Do not judge, so that you may not be judged. For with the judgment you make you will be judged, and the measure you give will be the measure you get. Why do you see the speck in your neighbor's eye but do not notice the log in your own eye." (Matt 7:1-

3) Seeing the speck in our neighbor's eye is not an invitation to judge them but an opportunity to take responsibility for ourselves.

A second characteristic of nonjudgmental acceptance is detachment. When I step onto our patio and watch a sunset, I do not try to change it. I am not attached to a particular way every beautiful sunset should look. I do not say, "Can I have a little more red over to the left?" or, "Please give me less of the pink to the south and some darker blue on the edge." If I am attached to a particular way every sunset should look, then I will always be judging sunsets against my own criteria. And I will almost certainly be disappointed by most sunsets rather than surprised by their unique beauty.

People are a lot like sunsets. I might want "a little more love, hope, and mercy over here and a little less greed and pride over there." But, in the end, I can no more change a person than I can change the sunset. Both simply are what they are. Only God can make them differently.

If I am attached to a particular picture of what people should do or who they should be, I am always going to be judging them as inadequate and imperfect. When I remain detached from any particular outcome, I do not need to evaluate what is missing and then impose what I think "ought to be." I can instead care about the other person and his or her agenda for what it is, with both its strengths and its limitations.

When coaches stay detached and nonjudgmental, they create a spaciousness in the coaching environment. This spaciousness allows room for truth and courage to emerge. In this environment, people discover room to vent anger or frustration or sorrow. People feel safe enough—in the presence of enough grace—to acknowledge their own guilt or shame. They do not feel confined by past judgments about what they can or cannot do, about what is or is not possible. This is hospitable space where people feel welcomed and accepted

The coach's nonjudgmental acceptance does not mean refraining from speaking the truth in love. Being judgmental or confrontational is not necessarily the same thing as confronting others with the truth. On the contrary, a stance of neutral detachment may be the only authentic basis for speaking the truth to someone else. Only when coaches are not attached to particular results or outcomes can they speak the truth to clients. The New Testament writers describe this as "speaking the truth in love." (Eph 4:15) The speaker is not attached to specific outcomes or interpretations. They are not in love with their own biases, prejudgments, or opinions. Only when coaches are not in love with their own truth can they speak the truth in love to their clients.

Telling the truth, from this perspective, is quite different than passing judgment—although people often confuse these terms with one another. Telling the truth means stating one's own experience or response without being attached to the results. Passing judgment, on the other hand, usually involves some attachment to particular commitments, actions, or outcomes.

Clients come to coaching because they want truthfulness. They recognize they are somehow stuck or bogged down but are unsure how to find their way forward. They are so caught in the fog of their own experience that they can no longer see the truth. They crave a place where they can speak truthfully about their lives and be spoken to truthfully. Coaching can be one place where people know they are not being judged but are instead being spoken to truthfully. In this space, people speak the truth in love: Honestly, straightforwardly, forthrightly, but without judgment.

This runs counter to our everyday social norms, which call for people to be pleasant and polite. Being polite usually entails avoiding anything that might confront people with embarrassing or painful truths. But clients do not pay their coaches to be polite. They want and deserve their coaches to speak the truth in love. Speaking truthfully is contagious. As coaches model how to speak the truth in love without any attachment to particular results, clients gradually discover they too can speak the whole truth about their lives.

Truthfulness requires great courage. It also releases tremendous energy. People usually tie up most of their energy for action in suppressing awareness and in avoidance. When the truth is finally told, a tidal wave of energy for positive action is unleashed. This released energy is the fuel that can power significant movement forward in people's lives.

Confidentiality. Safe space cannot exist without confidentiality. Confidentiality permits people to speak truthfully about their lives, knowing whatever they say in the coaching relationship will not go beyond it.

For people to change, they need the freedom to explore their assumptions. Examining these unspoken assumptions brings people face-to-face with embarrassing or even painful truths about themselves. Facing these limitations, fears, and doubts requires vulnerability. Confidentiality gives clients the freedom to make themselves vulnerable to the truth. They can share freely, without censoring their own thoughts. Without confidentiality, clients may not to be fully truthful with themselves or their coach. They are unlikely to discuss embarrassing, childish, or painful truths about themselves if they feel their coach may share these stories or comments with others.

When confidential information is shared outside the coaching relationship, coaches are participating in an age-old sin: gossip. "So also the tongue is a small member, yet it boasts of great exploits. How great a forest is set ablaze by a small fire. And the tongue is a fire." (Jas 3:5-6) Like gossip, sharing confidential information can do significant damage to people and their reputations.

Good ethical practice requires coaches to state explicitly their commitment to confidentiality. They need to say at the very beginning of the coaching relationship that everything within the coaching relationship remains confidential and then describe what confidentiality does and does not include.

For most coaches, confidentiality means keeping information given by or about an individual secure from others. Confidentiality requires that coaches do not disclose that a particular person is or has been in a coaching relationship without that person's explicit, written permission. It also includes not sharing comments, stories, or observations that are made by the client during coaching. The obligation to maintain confidentiality does not typically end when the client dies. Confidentiality also applies to all forms of communication: verbal, written, or electronic.

Coaches also need to be clear with potential clients that the coaching relationship does not have the same privileged status as some professional relationships. Communication between a priest and parishioner or an attorney and client, for example, are legally protected. But coaching conversations do not enjoy this legal protection of confidentiality. Clients need to know that the coach's commitment to confidentiality may not include illegal activities or remain protected in legal proceedings.

Nurturing Trust

Courageous space is also characterized by trust. All important relationships are ultimately established on a foundation of mutual trust. When trust breaks down, relationships usually suffer or even disintegrate. Without trust, coaches and clients cannot co-design a powerful alliance.

Trust is not independent of safety. Both trust and safety rely on many of the same qualities: truthfulness, confidentiality, and nonjudgmental acceptance. When coaches demonstrate confidentiality, they build trust in themselves as coaches. As they practice nonjudgmental acceptance, clients gain trust in the coaching alliance itself. Safety and trust mutually reinforce one another. People feel safe when they are around someone they trust. And, conversely, people experience others as trustworthy when they feel safe in their presence.

But trust is built on more than just safety. Some factors that contribute to trust are genuine concern for the client's best interests and goals, competence, integrity, and the sharing of power and control.

Genuine Concern for the Client. Every relationship involves risk. We risk that others are not acting in their own self-interest but are holding our interests to be as important as their own. Usually, when we violate someone's trust, they regard us as having acted in our own self-interest at their expense. Trust, in the coaching relationship, develops out of clients' knowledge that their coaches are genuinely concerned about their best interests. Their coaches will not put their own self-interest ahead of what is best for their clients. Clients depend on coaches not to do things that benefit them at the client's expense.

Genuine concern for the client also manifests itself in respect for the client's goals. Clients are willing to entrust themselves to the coaching alliance because they trust their coaches are not acting from narrow self-interest but out of concern for the client's goals. They quickly lose trust in the whole coaching relationship if they sense their coach is concerned primarily with himself or herself.

Competence. Competence refers to one's ability to use coaching tools, practices, and strategies. Coaches build trust as they demonstrate their proficiency in coaching skills, practices, and strategies. People have greater trust in a coach when they sense he or she is competent and adequately prepared. If, on the other hand, coaches act inconsistently or speak indecisively, people will question their trustworthiness. Such competence involves more than having a framed certificate on the wall. Competence is demonstrated through words and actions.

Integrity. Integrity encompasses several interpersonal characteristics, including consistency, predictability, and clear or transparent communication. People regard their coaches as trustworthy when they behave in predictable or consistent ways. They are not different people each time they meet with a client. They do what they say and say what they mean. They are not late for coaching appointments. They are not enthusiastic and engaged at one appointment, then distant and aloof in the next. If they make promises, they keep them.

Communication and trust are mutually reinforcing. Low trust and poor communication, on the other hand, create a downward spiral of misunderstanding and suspicion. If I distrust you, I am not likely to communicate clearly or directly, which further undermines our communication. Conversely, your direct communication fosters my trust; and I am therefore more likely to speak honesty with you, which further expands our circle of trust. If coaches speak candidly and forthrightly, truthfully and directly, clients will sense their trustworthiness.

Sharing Power and Control. Co-creating the coaching alliance builds trust. Designing this alliance makes clear that the client is always in control of the goals and process of coaching. People are more apt to trust others when they do not feel there is a struggle for control happening between them. The more people sense someone is trying to control them or their agenda, the less willing they are to trust them. As coaches co-design the coaching relationship, they insure that control always remains with the client. The more clearly this is stated and acted upon, the more quickly the client can trust both the coach and the coaching relationship.

Second Task: The Initial Session

The first crucial opportunity to build a relationship of safety and trust is the initial session. During this session, the coach and client intentionally co-design their alliance. They explicitly negotiate the goals and parameters of their relationship. Although designing and re-designing the coaching relationship remains an ongoing task, it is especially important in the initial session.

The Initial Session

The initial session is the first scheduled appointment between a client and a coach. This session varies in length. They are usually longer than the normal coaching session. Some may last two or three hours. Most initial sessions cover several basic topics: getting acquainted, establishing coaching goals, logistics of coaching sessions, and orientation to basic coaching tools and practices.

Coaches and clients can underestimate the importance of this first session. They may want to hurry through it in order to get to the "meat of the coaching." They treat it as perfunctory, as a meaningless preliminary to real coaching. But I have frequently discovered that problems cropping up later in the coaching process can usually be traced back to mistakes made during this session. Taking time to become acquainted, establishing a clear focus for the coaching, discussing boundaries and logistics, and providing an introduction to key terms and tools will actually save time later in the coaching relationship.

Because this initial session can play such a pivotal role in co-designing the coaching alliance, many coaches send a welcome packet to clients before their first appointment. This packet includes a welcome letter outlining what will happen during the session. It also includes several forms or questionnaires, which the client completes and returns prior to the appointment. (See Sample 5.1)

Learning Who The Client Is

Coaches use the intake session to gather basic contact information: preferred and emergency telephone numbers, street addresses, email, or fax numbers. Some coaches gather additional information about birthdays, anniversaries, significant people or relationships in the client's life, and other personal data. (See Sample 5.2)

This portion of the initial session is also a time to hear about the client's life journey, particularly the experiences that have led him or her to seek out a coaching partnership. The objective is to begin to know the client from the inside out:

- What would a life that counts look like to you?
- Where do you get stuck when you try to make changes in your life?

Sample 5.1   Welcome Letter

Dear _____,

Welcome to coaching! I am looking forward to being your coach and helping you follow God more faithfully be living a life that becomes good news for you and for God's world.

Our coaching relationship exists for you—to help you learn faster and go farther than you otherwise would. We begin co-designing our coaching alliance with our first session from [time] until [time] on [date].

I'm sure you are as eager to begin as I am. To help us maximize our time during this initial appointment, I have enclosed some materials to complete and return to me before our appointment.
  • Personal Information Sheet
  • Getting to Know You Questions
  • Primary Focus Worksheet
Some of this information, such as the personal information form, will be very simple to complete. I hope you will give more time and thought to the Getting to Know You Questions and the Primary Focus Worksheet.

I am also including the Call Preparation Worksheet that we will use in future calls. You will not need to complete it before our initial appointment. As part of this appointment, I will explain how we will use it for future sessions.
  • Call Preparation Worksheet

During our initial conversation we will discuss the primary focus, logistics, and parameters of our coaching relationship. These will be developed into a formal covenant or agreement between us. Some information about the basic policies and procedures of this agreement is enclosed with this letter.
  • Sample Coaching Agreement

As you recall from our earlier conversation, the minimum time for our coaching relationship is three months. At the end of this period, we will have an opportunity to either conclude our coaching or renegotiate a new agreement. The fee for the intake appointment is $____. The fee for monthly coaching is $____. We will work together for four 30-minute sessions each month. I send invoices on the 20th of each month and expect payment prior to the first of each mont.

I am looking forward to working together with you on [time and date]. Please call me at [telephone number].

Sincerely,

Sample 5.2   Sample Personal Information Form

PERSONAL INFORMATION SHEET

All personal information is confidential and will be treated as such.

Name:

Address:

Telephone Numbers

    Home: _____

    Office: _____

    Cell: _____

    Fax: _____

Email Address:

Personal Information

    Date of Birth: _____

    Significant People In Your Life:

    Special Days (birthday, anniversaries, holidays, etc.)

Occupational Information

    Position or Job Title:

    Employer:

Religious Information

        Membership:

        Offices or Ministries:

What are some other important facts or relationships or responsibilities that you feel I need to know?

- What are you expecting from me as your coach?
- What would life be like if you were fully living God's purposes for you?
- What are some ways that God made you a unique or special person?
- Who are some people that inspire you?
- When was a time you felt God was using you fully?
- What can I say or do when you are stuck to help you get moving again?
- What might I do or say that would really drive you crazy?
- What are some tips you might give me about how you would like me to relate to you?

Some coaches may send these questions to the client before the initial session. (See Sample 5.3) The client then returns the form prior to the appointment. The completed questions provide a basis for conversation and exploration.

Sample 5.3 Getting To Know You Questions

GETTING TO KNOW YOU QUESTIONS

Please answer the questions below and fax or email your reponses to me before our intake appointment. All information is confidential and will be used only to help me learn more about you and how you would like me to be as your coach.

What would a life that counts look like to you?

Where do you get stuck when you try to make changes in your life?

What are you expecting from me as your coach?

What would life be like if you were fully living God's purposes for you?

What are some ways that God made you a unique or special person?

Who are some people that inspire you?

When was a time you felt God was using you fully?

What can I say or do when you are stuck to help you get moving again?

What might I do or say that would really drive you crazy?

What are some tips you might give me about how you would like me to relate to you?

What else would you like me to know about you?

Have you been or are you in therapy? If so, please describe your present relationship to a counselor or therapist and your experience of counseling.

Have you had or do you now have a formal spiritual director? If so, please describe your present relationship to your spiritual director and your experience of spiritual direction.

Some coaches also ask clients to complete a personality inventory. They may use instruments like the Myers-Briggs Type Inventory, the Herrmann Brain Dominance Instrument, the Strength Deployment Inventory, or DISC. This approach has certain risks. It may inadvertently communicate that there is a certain way the client "should" be. Seeing the results from these assessment instruments may also bias the coach toward certain conclusions about the client. Clients can sometimes use the results to avoid telling the truth. It is easier to say *That is just the way ESTJ's are* than to look at what really keeps them from taking certain actions or getting particular results in their lives.

These instruments also bring certain potential benefits to the coaching alliance if properly used. They can, for example, form a common framework for communication and relationship. I sometimes use the HBDI or Herrmann Brain Dominance Instrument with clients. In discussing the results, the client and I explore possible ways we might miscommunicate or misunderstand one another because we have different thinking styles. We then share how each of us likes to be communicated with and what comments or approaches cause us to shutdown. This conversation around our HBDI profiles creates a shared framework for communication between us.

Learning What the Client Wants

Clients and coaches need to have a clear picture of the relationship's primary focus: What actions does the client want to take? Where is the client trying to go? It is hard to achieve a poorly defined goal. Without a clear purpose, the coaching relationship runs the risk of losing its focus. The efforts of both coach and client can become diffused and disconnected.

Establishing clear goals also helps build trust. Having the client define his or her primary focus firmly plants the locus of control and responsibility where it belongs: with the client. The coaching alliance exists for the client. The client has to take ownership of this partnership from the very start if it is to be effective.

Some clients come with a well-defined focus already in mind. Others have difficulty describing the changes they are trying to make. They may know precisely what they want to stop doing; but they have only a fuzzy picture of the positive results they want. These clients need help clarifying the picture of what they are moving toward, not what they are escaping from.

Other clients may be tempted to over-commit. They have a long laundry list of actions that all seem equally important. They want to take on too many issues all at once. Coaches need to help these clients identify the three to five high-leverage outcomes that will make the most difference for their learning and performance.

Asking clients to write down three to five primary foci for coaching invites them to better define what they want from the coaching alliance. (See Sample 5.4) Coaches can ask clients to describe what successfully addressing these primary foci would look like. Being able to look back at this list and notice what has been accomplished serves to motivate clients. Reviewing this list helps both the client and coach assess how far they have come or what has been missing.

Sample 5.4 Primary Foci Worksheet

PRIMARY FOCUS WORKSHEET

Please list three to five primary areas you would like to work on in our coaching alliance. Use a short phrase to describe each primary focus. Then, below it, describe a measurable result for this focus.

EXAMPLE:

EFFECTIVELY LEAD SMALL GROUPS
I will have a system for preparing for each class session and a clearly defined lesson plan or learning design. .I will be confident of my skills in leading discussions that include everyone and stay on-track.

1.

2.

3.

4.

5.

Is This Client Right for My Coaching?

Coaches also use the initial session to assess whether a client is ready for coaching. If someone seems a poor candidate for coaching, the coach has a responsibility to discuss this concern with the client and to decide together what they might do next.

Questionable Clients. For example, I once had a client who, in the initial appointment, explained that she was leaving the country for an extended mission immersion experience. She would only be available for one month and would then be out-of-the-country for the next two months. She thought we could begin coaching, take a break, and resume when she returned. I explained that I only worked with clients if they could commit to three continuous months of coaching. I suggested she wait until she returned from her mission trip to begin her coaching. Although she pressed to begin immediately, I was firm in saying I could not coach her under these conditions.

When we finally did arrange for coaching subsequent to her trip, she said, "I see why you refused to start coaching before I left. This is really hard work. At first I was angry that you would not begin our coaching. Now, I am glad you did not give in."

Certain "red flags" may suggest that clients really need therapy, not coaching. In other cases, a potential client may be psychologically healthy but not ready for the high demands of coaching. If this is the case, the coach owes it to both the client and himself or herself to explore these issues with the client. Some questionable clients include those who:

- Show a passive deference to the coach
- Have a tendency to play it safe
- Are defensive
- Have unrealistic expectations about coaching

Some clients are too deferential. They are reluctant to state their goals and instead want the coach to tell them what to do. They defer to the coach and discount their own knowledge or experience.

I once had a client who had a long history of working as a consultant. He repeatedly responded to my comments by saying, "Of course, you are right. I should . . . ." He wanted me to function as the expert consultant who made recommendations about what he should do. At first, I tried to engage in some direct teaching about the differences between coaches and consultants. When the pattern kept repeating itself, I finally suggested that I was probably not the right coach to be working with him and we ended our relationship.

Other clients want to play it safe. They select low-risk goals and avoid taking on anything really big or challenging. These small steps do not fundamentally change anything but are easily achieved. Coaching, however, is for people who want to challenge themselves to go farther than they ever dreamed possible. They know that what God wants them to accomplish is so big they cannot do it alone. Coaching is for people who want to live a larger life that really counts. They do not just want to do the things that work; they want to do the things that count. Someone who avoids risks and wants to engage in small, incremental changes does not really need a coach.

Still other clients are defensive from the very beginning. They have an excuse for everything. They can give a thousand reasons for why nothing will change in their lives. They deny, blame, and rationalize. Coaching involves looking honestly at where people are stuck and how their own behavior is getting in the way of the results they want. People who cannot make themselves vulnerable enough to examine their lives truthfully are not ready for coaching.

Another group of people come to coaching with unrealistic expectations. They believe change and transformation will come quickly and easily. They think everything can be accomplished at once. These clients over-estimate their own strength, attention, and energy. Coaching is not a magic pill. It does not produce overnight results. No one can expect an ultra-fast microwave transformation of their lives. Real change happens in a slow cooking crock-pot. Clients who believe everything can be accomplished overnight are setting themselves up for disappointment and disillusionment.

Letting Go. If, in the course of the intake session, coaches discern that a particular client may not be a good fit, they need to discuss this topic honestly and truthfully. It is better to address one's concern directly during the initial session than to allow it to fester. When unaddressed, these issues typically result in subsequent frustrations and misunderstandings between coaches and clients.

Designing the Coaching Alliance

The initial session is an opportunity to review the logistics of coaching:

- How often will we have coaching appointments?
- How long will each session last?
- What happens if the client is late or misses an appointment?
- How long will our coaching relationship last? How is it ended?
- If payments are involved, how will they be handled?
- What boundaries or limits exist to the relationship?

Scheduling Appointments. Coaches follow different practices regarding the frequency and length of coaching appointments. As a general rule, coaching sessions are more flexible than the usual 50-minute weekly counseling session. One coach might schedule three 45-minute appointments each month with one week off. Another coach might schedule four 30-minute sessions per month. Many coaches keep their appointments via telephone, particularly if they are geographically separated from their clients. Others meet face-to-face. Coaches may even occasionally meet at their clients' workplaces to better understand their work environment, community context, or congregational climate.

This flexibility is rooted in the nature of the coaching process itself. Unlike counseling, where the therapeutic relationship is itself the primary context for healing, the coaching appointment is only one part of the over-all coaching process. Coaching is about actions, outcomes, and results. So most of the work is done between sessions as clients take action and reflect on what they learn from the results. The actual coaching session therefore can be more fluid and flexible. Whatever schedule of appointments coaches and clients agree upon, both parties need to be clear that this time is inviolate. Clients who commit to a schedule and then perpetually have conflicts or cancellations are really saying they are not fully committed to their coaching partnership.

Boundaries to the Relationship. Coaches and clients also need clear agreements about their relationship's boundaries and what consequences occur when boundaries are violated. Most coaches allow for some contact via email or fax between appointments. There are limits to this availability, however. Clients should not call or email between appointments to gather information they could easily glean for themselves. Similarly, clients ought not to use their coach as an emergency responder. Coaches are not a "4-1-1" or "9-1-1" service. When this happens, clients are failing to take responsibility for their own learning and growth. Coaches need to promptly address such boundary violations.

Coaches and clients also need to agree on what happens if clients are late or miss appointments. If a client is chronically late or regularly misses appointments without prior notice, the coach needs to address this behavior directly and in a nonjudgmental way. He or she can describe the pattern, indicate its impact on the coaching, and then ask what the client's behavior means. If the behavior continues, the coach may need to terminate the relationship.

The same principle applies to payments. If the coach is charging for his or her services, then clients need to know when payments are due. Both coach and client also need to understand what will happen if payments are missed or chronically late.

The initial session is an appropriate time to discuss the expected length of the coaching relationship. Significant change is hard work. It will not happen in one week or even one month. The coaching relationship should be long enough for new behaviors and learning to take root in clients' lives. In addition, most clients experience a slump about six or eight weeks into coaching. They may initially make rapid progress. Then, more deeply engrained patterns pull them back into old habits. Their long-term relationship systems attempt to re-establish the old homeostasis, forcing them back into old roles and behaviors. At this point, clients can become discouraged or disappointed. At the precise moment when they are on a transformational threshold and need coaching the most, they are the most tempted to quit.

Most coaches consequently insist on a three-month commitment. A minimum commitment of three months ensures that clients stay with the coaching partnership long enough to achieve and sustain new learning and performance.

How the relationship ends or is re-negotiated after this initial three-month period is another topic for the intake session. Clients and coaches need to agree on how the relationship will conclude or continue. They may also want to discuss some signs that the relationship needs to be completed early and how the coach or client introduces this topic.

Formulating an Explicit Coaching Agreement

Coaches formalize these discussions into a written agreement. Both the coach and the client keep signed, dated copies. The coach's attorney should review the basic template for this agreement to ensure the coach is legally protected. (See Sample 5.5) Topics in this agreement include:

- Confidentiality agreements
- A clear statement that coaching is not a substitute for therapy and the coach is not a mental health professional.
- A clear statement that coaching is not legal or financial advising and the client should consult with a legal or financial professional before taking actions that might have important legal or financial implications.
- A direct statement that the client remains responsible for all actions she or he might take as a result of coaching.
- A definition of the time period over which coaching will occur.
- A statement of the length, day, and number of monthly sessions.
- A description of when the client will make payments for coaching services and what these payments will be.
- A summary statement of the primary focus for the coaching: What are the main topics the client wants to address with the coach?

Throughout the coaching process, coaches will be educating clients about coaching strategies and techniques. They will also be teaching clients about particular coaching terms. The initial appointment is an appropriate time to introduce some of the key tools and strategies they will be using.

One unique characteristic of coaching is its emphasis on action. People come to coaching because they want things to be different in their lives. They want results. Accountability for results, therefore, plays a major role in the coaching conversation. When a client identifies an action or agrees to coaching homework between sessions, the coach will ask for how the client plans to be accountable for these actions. The coach usually asks:

- What actions are you going to take?
- What is your timeline for these actions?; and
- How do you want to let me or others know when you have completed these actions?

In addition to explaining what accountability is and how it works, coaches will want to define another commonly used strategy: Requesting. Coaches need to have permission to request that client's take particular actions, which they think may enhance learning or move the client further toward his or her goals. When a coach makes a request, the client can make one of three responses:

- "Yes"
- "No"
- "My counteroffer is. . . "

Coaches also use the initial session to talk about the over-all flow of the coaching process. Clients need to know that coaching includes times of both progress and resistance. As clients come closer to significant breakthroughs, other forces will push back against these changes. This process of resistance often leads to a slump or low-point about six or eight weeks into the coaching relationship. If clients understand this slump and the process of resistance, they are better equipped to stay the course.

Finally, coaches may want to discuss specifically what resistance looks like in the client's life. Most of us have tried to move forward in our lives before. But we usually sabotage our own best intentions. We fall back into old habits of self-limiting judgments. Coaching is about having a powerful context for finally changing this pattern. Precisely because coaching seeks to break through these patterns of self-sabotage, they will show up with a certain and inevitable fierceness.

Sample 5.5 Coaching Agreement

COACHING AGREEMENT

This agreement between [Name] and [Name] begins on [Date] and continues until [Date]. The client understands that coaching is designed to facilitate his/her creation of goals and a plan for achieving these goals. He/she also understands that coaching is a comprehensive partnership that can involve many areas of life. The client always remains responsible for how these areas will be incorporated into the coaching.

The coach and client will meet as follows: [Day of Week] from [Time] to [Time] for [Number of Sessions] per month. The client will call the coach at [Telephone Number] and will pay for all long-distance charges, if any. Client and coach agree to give each other 24 hours notice if either party needs to cancel or reschedule a coaching session. The client may call or email the coach between sessions if needed.

The fee for the intake appointment is $_____. The fee for monthly coaching is $_____. Invoices are sent on the 20th of each month and payment is expected prior to the first day of each month. If the client is unable to pay, he/she and the coach will discuss an alternative payment plan. Nonpayment may result in termination of the coaching agreement.

When this initial three-month coaching agreement ends, client and coach will discuss whether to discontinue coaching or renegotiate a new agreement. If, at any point, either the coach or the client feels it is time to complete the coaching relationship, they may bring this topic to the next coaching session. The relationship will terminate two weeks after notice of termination is given.

The coach promises that all information and the fact that we are in a coaching relationship will be held confidential to the extent permitted by law, unless the client directs the coach otherwise in writing. The coach would be required to inform an appropriate professional if the client intended to physically harm himself/herself or someone else. The coaching relationship is not considered "privileged" under the law such as one would have with a lawyer, therapist, spouse, or religious counselor.

The initial session is a great opportunity to remind clients that these self-limiting patterns will eventually show up in the coaching relationship. Coach and client can then explore what these forces look like in the client's life. This conversation naturally moves into a discussion about how the client wants the coach to work with these patterns and habits.

Client understands that this coaching relationship is being established for the sole purpose of helping the client achieve his/her personal and professional goals. These goals are

- [Primary Focus]
- [Primary Focus]
- [Primary Focus]

In no way should coaching be construed as psychological counseling, psychotherapy, medical advice, or any type of therapy or counseling. Coaching does not involve diagnosis or treatment of any mental disorder defined by the American Psychiatric Association. The client understands that coaching is not a substitute for any kind of mental health care or substance abuse treatment. If the client feels that he/she needs professional counseling or therapy, it is his/her responsibility to seek it. If the client is receiving mental health care or substance abuse treatment, he/she agrees to disclose this to both the therapist and the coach and to have consulted with his/her therapist about the advisability of coaching. The client also understands that coaching is not professional legal or financial advice and will seek appropriate professionals before taking action in these areas.

By entering into this agreement, the coach does not guarantee that any specific results will be achieved. The client at all time remains entirely responsible for whatever actions he/she takes and the consequences of those actions. It is the coach's intention to honor the agenda the client brings, to help the client move forward but not to lead or direct. The direction comes from you, the client.

_____

Client's Signature   Date

_____

Coach's Signature   Date

THE INITIAL APPOINTMENT'S IMPLICIT GOAL

The initial session has several goals: Gather information about the client, clarify the primary focus for the coaching relationship, design the coaching relationship's boundaries and logistics; teach the client about basic coaching tools. All these objectives are ultimately secondary to the initial session's primary goal, however.

As clients and coaches co-design their alliance and co-create an agenda, clients are learning what it means to be full partners in their own learning and growth. This full partnership is the bedrock upon which everything else in the coaching relationship is built. If the coach conveys nothing else during the initial session except this basic sense of a shared partnership designed to benefit the client's learning and growth, he or she will have succeeded.

Third Task: Connecting Purpose to Results

This is the third and longest stage in the coaching relationship. Coaches help clients stay connected to their sense of purpose as they take action. There is often an inverse relationship between busyness and clarity of purpose. The less clear we are about our purpose, the busier we become. The more we throw ourselves into activity after activity, the fuzzier our vision may be. Coaches play a crucial role in helping clients both take action and stay focused on what is important in their lives.

During this stage, the coach and client move from a problem-orientation to a vision-orientation. This task usually begins by supporting clients as they clarify their values and vision of God's call to ministry. Clarity about values and vision allows clients to align their actions with their vision. Powerful actions flow out of a clear picture of who they are as God's creation and what God is seeking to accomplish through them. The goal is not to define what is wrong with the client's life. It is to paint a compelling picture of the future into which God is calling the client to move.

The client and coach are also working on concrete steps that will move the client toward this future. The overt goal of this action planning is to keep the client moving forward. The implicit goal is to reinforce continually that the client—not the coach—is responsible for his or her own action and learning.

During this phase, coaches help their clients explore possibilities outside their normal assumptions. Coaches challenge, probe, and confront. They support clients as they step beyond their previous comfort zones. They challenge them to identify the knowledge, skills, attitudes, and habits they need to take action in God's service.

Coaches also help clients come face-to-face with their self-limiting judgments, sabotage, and resistance. People often become most stuck when they are on the threshold of achieving what they most desire. People know intuitively that achieving their God's purposes for their lives will mean letting go of familiar habits, excuses, and attitudes. Sometimes it is easier to hold onto these familiar ways than embrace the unknown. The coach's task is to help people face their own resistance and self-sabotage in creative and courageous ways so that clients finally step over the threshold of transformation.

During this middle and longest stage, coaches and clients pay careful attention to actions that will create the envisioned future while simultaneously deepening the client's self-understanding and learning. The coaching relationship provides a safe setting where clients can discover the courage to persist in the concrete details, priorities, and action steps with which they are engaged.

Fourth Task: Coming to Closure

Coming to closure in the coaching relationship represents a major challenge for both the coach and the client. Usually, the seeds of closure are sown much earlier than the actual closure itself. Coaches and clients plant these seeds when they design the initial coaching agreement during the initial session. This agreement usually includes a description of the minimum length of the coaching relationship and how closure will be negotiated. Discussions about closure can be less emotionally charged when the initial coaching agreement discussed how the partnership will be completed.

Closure is typically an evolving process. It is also beset with uncertainty and surprises. Relationships may end early because of unexpected events. Family crises or medical emergencies can redirect a client's time and energy. Sometimes coaching relationships can last longer than they should. A client may have become comfortable in the relationship and not want it to end. A sense of inertia can overtake both coach and client. Neither party wants to bring up how the learning has gone flat and the action has lost momentum.

A number of signs indicate that it is time for closure. The coach needs to be alert for these signs and discuss them with the client. One sign that the relationship is nearing completion is the accomplishment of the client's primary objectives. Clients may have come to coaching with things they needed to accomplish in their lives. They have now realized these original goals and the clients' energies are going into consolidation rather than creation.

Clients may also have come to coaching for a new perspective on their lives. They find they have made significant progress in learning to understand their assumptions, habits, and skills. They have moved from reaction to self-direction. They have strengthened their muscles for action-reflection and learning. They have a new-found grasp of their strengths and capacities. Now, they are ready to build on these competencies without the ongoing support of a coaching relationship.

Other, less positive reasons can sometimes signal that the coaching partnership is completed. One or both parties may feel their alliance is not contributing to progress on the issues. Coach or client may finish each session feeling drained and exhausted rather than energized. They may sense the other person resents them or begrudges them the time invested in the coaching. One party may begin missing appointments or habitually showing up late. Some designed alliances fizzle out. Others degenerate into missed opportunities, boredom, and resentment.

It is never appropriate for one party or the other to just walk away. It leaves unfinished business for both the coach and client. When it feels like time for closure, coaches need to discuss this topic with their clients. Some steps in the closure process are:

- State what you are experiencing about the need for closure. This may be based on the original timeline stated in the coaching agreement. It can also arise from what has or has not been happening in the coaching relationship. If there is a problem, acknowledge it without casting blame or passing judgment.
- Revisit the original purpose for the coaching alliance: What was the primary focus? What was the goal for working together?
- Review what has happened. When were you most scared? When did you feel most exhilarated? When did you most surprise yourself or others? What was a turning point or critical "Aha!" moment? What worked best? What did not work? What was missing?
- Celebrate the learning and action that has taken place. What has the client learned about himself? What has she achieved or accomplished that was unexpected? How is he a different person? What will she do to apply what she has learned? How will he keep building his new skills, knowledge, and attitudes?
- Negotiate the next phase of the relationship. Some coaches suggest they continue to meet on an infrequent basis, particularly if the alliance has worked well. The coach and client might negotiate a quarterly or annual check-in session. If the relationship is terminating on a less positive note, the coach might make a referral. He or she would usually give to the client the names of two or three coaches who might be well suited for this particular client. The coach and client can also discuss how they will handle future social interactions. What will their response be if they are together on a church committee or at a social event?

The Flow of a Coaching Session

Coaching is an art, not a science. There is no "add water and mix" formula for coaching. It cannot be reduced to an easy three-step process. At its core, coaching is a relationship that exists for the client's agenda. So the coach always follows where the client's agenda goes. As clients and coaches dance in the present moment, the client's agenda always leads.

Nonetheless, coaches can help people go farther and learn faster if they have some general format for each coaching session. (See Figure 5.2) The relative weight and importance of each component will vary with individual clients. Yet having a general outline of where one begins and how one concludes each session can guide both the coach and the client through the coaching conversation.

Pre-Appointment Preparations

The coaching appointment does not begin when the telephone rings or the client walks through the door. Coaching sessions are effective when both the coach and the client come prepared.

Figure 5.2 The Flow of a Coaching Session

Step One	Preparing	How do I want to show up at this appointment? What do I need to pray about? What is the core issue?
Step Two	Starting Quickly	Begin on time Intrude
Step Three	Reflecting on Action and Learning	Reporting on previous homework + What did you do? + What worked? + What didn't work? + What is missing? + What did you learn?
Step Four	Refocusing and Planning	Do I have the right perspective? What mental model am I tied to? What might better serve me? What is next? What is my plan for getting there?
Step Five	Reviewing and Closure	How do you want to be held accountable for your commitments? What do we need to pray about? What notes do I need to make about this session?

Effective coaches review their notes and have a plan for their session. During each appointment, the coach should keep careful notes about what the client is saying. Writing down the client's exact words helps them refresh their memory and see connections between conversation topics. Coaches should also note what they do not hear the client saying: What is the client avoiding? In what ways is she holding back? Denying his power? Reviewing notes from previous sessions also reminds coaches of the client's primary focus and agenda. This can keep a coach from becoming lost in side issues and minor details.

Clients also have work to do before their coaching appointment. They complete a Coaching Preparation Worksheet and email or fax it to their coach prior to the session. (See Sample 5.6) This worksheet is usually included in the welcome packet. Then, during the initial session, the coach explains how it will be used. This form might ask:

- What actions have you taken that you want to celebrate?
- What is still missing after your last actions?
- What happened differently from what you expected?
- What did you set as a goal that you have not done?

Sample 5.6 Coaching Call Preparation Form

COACHING PREPARATION WORKSHEET

Please complete this form and fax or email it to me no later than two hours before our coaching session.

What actions have you taken that you want to celebrate?

What is challenging you now?

What is still missing after your last step?

What happened differently from what you expected?

What did you set as a goal that you have not done?

What is next for you?

What do you want from this coaching session?

How do you need me to coach you in this session?

How can I be praying for you and your situation?

- What is next for you?
- What do you want from this coaching session?
- How do you need me to coach you in this session?
- How can I be praying for you and your situation?

The Coaching Preparation Worksheet serves both the coach and the client. When clients complete this form, they show up for the appointment more centered and focused on key topics. Because the coach has the client's responses prior to the session, he or she can show up better prepared for the session.

Opening Up – Getting to the Point Quickly

Most coaching sessions are brief, especially when compared to the 50-minute counseling hour. Many coaches have 30-minute appointments on a weekly basis. The briefer session means that clients and coaches must be concise and to the point. The coaching appointment, unlike a therapeutic session, moves at a fast pace.

This is one reason for the Coaching Preparation Worksheet. Having clients complete a preparation worksheet helps them focus on what they really want from this appointment. Clients will have already identified key learnings and actions. They will be less inclined to tell stories and ramble if they have given thought to what they want as the session's focus.

Permission to Intrude

This fast-paced conversation gives the coach permission to engage in a behavior that would not normally occur in social situations: Intruding.

Clients often want to use the coaching session to tell stories. They may believe the story gives background or explains some deeper truth. At another level, telling stories serves a different, often unconscious purpose. It allows people to appear to be saying something important while they are actually avoiding the real issue. If I *tell* a story about a situation, I don't have to *do* anything about it. Clients may also bring the expectation—probably shaped by experiences with counselors—that if they tell a story, then the coach will give them its interpretation or meaning.

Coaching, however, is about action and learning. Coaches do not give expert diagnoses of events. Therapists may listen stories about the past; but coaching is forward-oriented. It is about what clients will do in the future, not what happened in the past. So coaches need to intrude on their client's stories and ask them to get to the point. When a client begins to ramble or drift into a story, the coach can intrude and ask for the bottom line. Asking for the bottom line means asking for the essence or meaning behind the story rather than the whole story itself. The client needs to state the meaning or truth, not the coach. Intruding need not be rude; but it does keep the conversation focused. Since intruding breaks many of our normal social rules, coaches need to explain how and why they are using this skill.

BEGIN AND END ON TIME

Because the time is limited and focused, clients and coaches share equal responsibility for starting and ending on time. Clients who are perpetually late in keeping their appointments need to know that additional time will not be extended beyond the agreed-upon ending. Coaches are less likely to allow clients to ramble and tell stories if they know they must end at the designated time. Some coaches schedule back-to-back appointments to discipline themselves to end their sessions on time, even if clients have arrived late or have been allowed to ramble off-topic.

Reflecting on Learning And Action

Coaches help people think about themselves and their ministries more clearly. They provide support, encourage reflection-in-action, and hold clients accountable for the decisions they make. These tasks establish the flow of most coaching conversations.

If the previous coaching appointment ended with some homework, asking about these assignments is usually the best starting point. What can they celebrate as having achieved? What happened differently than they expected? What is still missing in spite of taking action? In what ways did they not follow through with their plans?

Clients can learn from their failures to act. The objective is not to shame clients or allow them to wallow in guilt and self-pity. Looking at their failure to follow-through on commitments can yield important insights into what keeps them stuck or bogged down where they are. What got in the way of taking action? What were the messages they told themselves about taking or not taking action? What does their lack of follow-through say about how they deal with other issues? If they are not committed to this action, what are they really committed to?

Part of the reason coaching works is clients know that their coach will be asking them what they have done and what results have they achieved. This basic accountability for action serves to keep people focused and moving toward their goals. Clients often say that they have never been so focused and able to stay on target with their goals.

Refocusing And Planning

The next portion of the coaching session asks the question: What is next? Coaches and clients refocus the conversation on what clients will do next and what concrete plans they will adopt. To answer the question of next steps, clients need to recognize how their assumptive frameworks and mental models may be getting in the way of the results they want. Perhaps the most difficult part of refocusing is helping clients realize they have choices about the way they look at the world. They can choose another perspective on their situation that will enable them to see other opportunities and actions.

When clients look at the results they achieved from previous actions, they become aware of their assumptions and hidden perspectives. Once these are out in the open, clients can more critically examine them. When people are bogged down in their life or work, it is usually because they have narrowed their perspective and cannot see or think about themselves or their situation in another way.

Our most hidden assumptions about "the way we ought to be" or "the way things are" pop into clearest view when events do not follow our assumed script. We all have assumptions about cause-and-effect. "If we do this, then that will happen." Or "We cannot act this way because they will do that." So if we do the unexpected, what really does happen? Probably not what we anticipated. So where did our rule about what "ought" to happen come from? And does it really serve our best interest any longer? Do we need another rule of thumb that will serve our desired results better?

A narrow perspective both blinds and binds us. Seeing reality from only one angle blinds us to other viable alternatives. The more we see no perspective but our own, the more tightly bound we become to that narrow way of thinking and acting. This shrinking perspective on our selves and our situations also undercuts our resilience. We have no place to which we can retreat or where we can recover our objectivity. We become trapped in a vicious cycle of anxiety and fear. The more we depend on one narrow perspective, the more anxious we become about the relevance, reliability, and truth of this perspective. The more anxious we are, the more difficult it becomes for us to loosen our grip on this cherished perspective and see beyond it to other possibilities.

Coaches help clients work through these vicious cycles of narrowing perspectives that bind and blind. The coaching space is where people can find the courage to face the anxieties that have blinded and bound them. It is where clients can realize they are not as bound as they have believed. They are free. They do have a choice. They can choose whether to remain committed to this narrow perspective or to embrace some new mental models that provide better road maps for their lives.

Past choices ought not to become a prison that limits people. Just because they made one choice at earlier point in their lives does not mean they permanently gave up their power of choice. They are not victims of their past choices. They cannot say, "I chose to take this job, so I cannot . . . " Or "Because I chose to take on this responsibility at church, I have to . . . "

From this place of choice about one's perspective, clients find the freedom to brainstorm alternative ways of looking at their situations. Once clients have committed themselves freely to another choice or option, coaches can guide them in developing an action plan, identifying resources, and creating structures that help maintain commitment and accountability.

Reviewing And Closure

As the coaching session comes to an end, the coach may want to review key points in the conversation. What are the main insights or new learnings the client has gained? What commitments to action has the client made? Are their requests or challenges that the client accepted? How does the client want to be held accountable for these next steps?

Either at this point or immediately after the coaching appointment, the coach will want to make careful notes about the client's assignments, homework, or action steps. These commitments create the starting point for the next coaching session. Coaches need a system of notes and files that works for them. (See Sample 5.7) I use an 8½ x 11 sheet for each coaching appointment. The client's name and date are at the top of this page. In the first section, I write key comments, metaphors, or phrases. In the second section I list key learnings and results the client has achieved. Then, in the last section, I summarize homework assignments, action steps, and accountability agreements. Each sheet—plus the client's pre-appointment coaching worksheet—is placed in the file on top of the previous session's notes and worksheet. With this system, I can quickly look at a file and see what happened the previous week as well as the longer-term issues that we have discussed.

Avoiding Rigid Formulas for the Coaching Session

Coaching would be pretty boring and dry if each session followed the same cookie-cutter format. The reality is always much more messy. Sometimes, coaches and clients work several sessions to name the primary focus and clarify what the

Sample 5.7 Session Notes

COACHING SESSION NOTES

Name:
Date:

Key comments, metaphors, phrases used repeatedly, or things that were <u>not</u> said/spoken

Important Learnings or Insights

Homework

    Commitment to Action:
    When Accomplished:
    How Will I Know?:

---

client wants or to paint a compelling picture of the future. Many times, several sessions will be spent trying to loosen the grip of a particularly narrow and deeply rooted perspective. How tasks are distributed over time depends, in part, upon the developmental cycle discussed in Chapter Two. A client entering in the Re-Examination substage of Self-Renewal will be asking different questions than someone who is in the Building the Future substage of Engagement.

Because each coach and every client are unique human beings, no simple formula works for every situation. Coaches instead follow the client's lead in establishing the pace and flow of coaching conversations. Beneath this rhythm and flow of dialogue, both parties are prayerfully listening for the Spirit's guidance as they build their coaching partnership.

CHAPTER SIX

THE COACH AS CATALYST

A chemical catalyst is an agent, usually present in a small amount, that initiates or accelerates the release of new energies from other chemicals. Like a chemical catalyst, coaches initiate or accelerate the release of energy in clients' lives. Catalysts are not changed by the chemical reactions they unleash. In the same way, coaches unleash clients to make envisioned changes in their lives without getting in their way or being used up in the process.

Coaches use several strategies to release or accelerate transformative energy. These include:

- Skillful listening
- Catalytic questioning
- Telling the truth
- Asking permission
- Requesting
- Challenging

This chapter will explore these skills and their use in the coaching alliance.

Skillful Listening

Listening is an essential ingredient for effective coaching. It serves as a fundamental building block for every other coaching skill or tool. If coaches cannot listen skillfully, their conversations will fall flat and feel empty.

Human beings interact in many ways. Look beneath all of them and you will find speech. Speech is one of the primary ways human beings relate to each other. Speaking and listening are thus absolutely fundamental to human identity. To listen is to acknowledge the other person as worthy of attention. To feel genuinely heard is a transformative experience. Nothing is more life-changing and energizing than to have another person authentically listen to us. Listening can be an experience of grace.

Listening and being heard constitute one of the Bible's most enduring themes. To listen is a gift of grace we bestow in the name of Jesus Christ: "Every generous act of giving, with every perfect gift, is from above . . . You must understand this, my beloved: let everyone be quick to listen, slow to speak, and slow to anger." (Jas 1:17, 19) Consequently, one expression of human sin is the failure to listen: "Hear this, O foolish and senseless people, who have eyes, but do not see, who have ears, but do not hear." (Jer 5:21)

When coaches listen, they suspend memory, judgment, and desire. Suspending memory means being fully present. People cannot be truly present when their minds are elsewhere, preoccupied by other thoughts. Effective coaches are not thinking about their personal to-do list when clients are speaking. They do not allow people's comments to trigger private introspection on their own experiences or memories. They are not reminiscing about their vacation or thinking about what to fix for dinner. Their minds are not somewhere other than with their clients. They are fully present and attentive to the other person's communication.

When coaches listen, they suspend judgment as well as memory. They do not listen to give advice. They do not listen to disagree. They listen to understand. Judging increases one's sense of power over another person. People place themselves "one-up" when they pass judgment. This makes them feel great. Unfortunately, it also increases the client's sense of powerlessness. Coaching is not about the coach's feeling powerful and in control. It involves clients experiencing more fully the Spirit's power. It is not about the client surrendering his or her power to the coach but instead about receiving the power of God's Spirit.

Most church leaders have learned to listen for what is wrong. They have succeeded in ministry by pointing out others' errors and demonstrating that they have the right answer. Coaching requires something entirely different. Listening for what is wrong will not serve a client's agenda. To become a good coach, church leaders and Christian educators need to stop listening for what is wrong. Coaching involves listening for people's greatness, not their smallness.

When coaches suspend judgment, they let their clients possess their own experience. Suspending judgment means going out of oneself and entering into the client's experience. For a few moments, coaches exist for and with the other person.

In doing so, they give clients permission to expand their view of reality rather than invalidate it.

Once people truly feel heard, they can usually stop defending what they see as their truth and entertain other viewpoints. They are more willing to entertain other perspectives when they feel someone has truly entered into the truth of their own experience and understood it. By listening to their clients, coaches validate clients' perceptions and thus make it possible for them to stop defending and begin questioning how they look at the world. When this happens, clients leave feeling clearer in their own minds, more aware of other possibilities, empowered to act.

When coaches listen, they also suspend desire. Suspending desire means remaining detached from any particular outcome, solution, or result. When coaches suspend desire, they are not listening for "the solution" to a client's situation. They do not impose their own goals on the client. Listening for a solution undermines effective coaching because it blocks the process of creativity and discovery. Once coaches become attached to solutions, they stop listening, discovering, or co-creating with their clients.

Some guidelines for skillful listening include the following. (See Figure 6.1)

Come to the Coaching Session Prepared to Listen

Remove other distractions from your workspace. Put away papers or projects you have been working on. A flickering computer screen, an unfinished report, a recent book, or a newly arrived email can take you away from being fully present. In the momentary glance at something else, clients intuitively know that coaches are not focusing 100 percent on them.

I was sitting in a restaurant talking about an important project with an acquaintance. His cellphone rang. Immediately he answered it. The message was clear: I was less important than someone he did not even know. Everyone has had this experience. People break their connection with us to answer the phone, wave, glance at a fax, or fiddle with their email. What is the subtle message they are communicating? Anything else is more important than being with you.

We live in a world that encourages multitasking. Seldom do we give our full attention to only one person or task. We talk on the phone and check our email. We write a quick memo while driving our car. If we are coaching over the telephone, we may think we can check our email or surf the web while our client is talking. Think again. Clients intuitively know whether or not they have our full attention.

Let the Other Person Do the Talking

Most successful leaders got where they are by speaking up. Leadership, they have come to believe, involves taking charge of the discussion. One way to be in control of a conversation is to dominate the air-time. Whoever does all the talking covertly controls the relationship. This approach will not work in the coaching alliance. Effective coaching requires good listening, not effective speech-making. As a coach, I monitor how often I am talking. If I talk for more than 20 percent of a coaching session, then I am probably talking too much. My goal is to listen clients into speech. It is not to let them know my opinions and thoughts. As clients talk, they come to their own discoveries and reach their own solutions. If I speak too much, I interfere with their creativity. The more I speak, the more I drift into giving advice or letting my opinions be known. My talking keeps clients from hearing themselves think aloud. It deprives them of the opportunity to discover their own insights and clarify their own hidden biases. By talking too much, I take power away from the client.

Wait Until the Other Person Finishes Their Thoughts Before You Respond

Sometimes people interrupt because they want to be in control. At other times, people interrupt because they believe they already know what the client is going to say. Yet, even when coaches finish clients' thoughts for them, they never really know what they want to say. A coach should not be constantly poised for rebuttal or response. By letting clients finish without being interrupted, coaches create space for clients to have their own thoughts and make their own discoveries.

Take Notes

Writing down key phrases or metaphors helps coaches stay focused on important themes and issues. If the coaching appointment is face-to-face, it also lets clients know their coach thinks what they are saying is important. Do not take too many notes, however. The coaching session is not a college lecture hall. Writing too much can distract both coach and client.

Listen for Both Facts and Feelings

Powerful coaching arises from listening with the ears and the eyes and the emotions. Coaches are not just listening to their client's words. They are also listening to their client's emotional tone. If they have co-designed a powerful alliance, coaches have an intuitive connection with their clients. Their own feelings and emotions then provide important clues about what clients are communicating. Coaches also listen to the non-verbal clues in the environment. What is the energy level in the room? What is the tone of voice saying? What just happened when the client's vocal energy dropped or spiked suddenly? Does the emotional tone match the words? If not, what does the incongruity suggest?

Paraphrase and Mirror

Let the client know you are listening by paraphrasing or mirroring. When we paraphrase, we re-state in our own words what we have heard the other person say and then check if our understanding is correct. When we mirror, we use exact words or phrases the client is speaking and check for understanding. Paraphrasing and mirroring let the client know they are understood. Sometimes clients ramble or repeat themselves because they do not believe they have been heard. By paraphrasing and mirroring, coaches let clients know they have been heard. They then do not feel obliged to repeat their thoughts one more time hoping someone will understand them.

Be Comfortable with Silence

Most of us are uncomfortable in a relationship if no one is speaking. We treat silence as rejection or judgment. Silence can make us anxious. Faced with silence, we may feel no one is in control of the relationship. As a consequence, most people blurt something out just to end the anxiety-laden silence. This discomfort with silence can be a barrier to effective coaching. Coaches need to be comfortable with silence. By speaking too soon because of their own discomfort, coaches let clients evade responsibility for their own learning and growth. Clients may unconsciously think that if they remain quiet long enough, the coach will reveal the truth of their experience or tell them what to do. The coaching conversation exists for the sake of the client's thoughts, ideas, insights, and puzzlements. Not the coach's. Coaches need to embrace silence. If they wait long enough, clients will usually grow equally uncomfortable with the same silence and speak up just to end their own discomfort!

Catalytic Questioning

Listening is a necessary but insufficient condition for calling a conversation "coaching." The strategic power of any coaching conversation resides in the coach's

Figure 6.1 Listening Skills for Coaches

ability to ask good questions. Powerful, catalytic questions release a client's best thinking. A good question acts as a catalyst for surfacing hidden issues. It focuses or re-focuses a client's tentative course of action. It inspires honest assessment and analysis. planning and follow-through. Coaching's effectiveness depends on powerful questions that propel clients toward deeper self-awareness and more responsible action. (See Figure 6.2)

A well-placed question arises out of skillful listening. If coaches are not listening to their clients, they cannot hear the client's own unspoken questions. A catalytic question restates in a clear and powerful way what the client has already been asking but did not know it.

Not all questions are created equal, however. Some questions open up possibilities. Others close off dialogue. A good question focuses awareness on one's own experience. It allows someone to probe more deeply

Good Questions are Value-Neutral

A good question is value-neutral. Coaches avoid communicating their own opinions or advice in the form of a question. Clients know the answer is "yes" when coaches ask: *Do you think you could improve your Christian education ministry by hiring a youth director?* Clients know the answer is "no" if their coaches say: *Do you think you really need to hire a consultant to help the congregation decide whether to add a second worship service?*

Never insert words like *really* or *actually* into questions. These words are like a neon light. They immediately convey to the client that the coach already has an opinion. As, for example, in questions such as: *You are not actually going to hire a new music director, are you?* or *Do you really think forming a youth council is a good idea?*

Good Questions are Positive

Catalytic questions are constructive and positive. They keep clients focused on the future rather than in the past. Questions such as *What happened to the children's ministry that got it to this point?* look backward. Archeology may be helpful if you are teaching an adult Sunday school class on the Old Testament. But it is not helpful in the coaching conversation. It does not really matter how the children's ministry arrived at its current condition. What matters is where the client wants this ministry to go and what he or she can do as a next step forward.

Positive questions focus on the future. They ask where the client wants to go, not what they are trying to leave behind. A world of difference exists between the question *How can you get people to stop skipping Church Council meetings?* and *What would make your Church Council meeting so exciting people would not want to miss one?*

Good Questions Avoid "Why?"

Coaches should be especially cautious in using one particular type of question. *Why* questions almost always make people defensive. *Why* questions evoke self-justification and guarded responses. They almost never send people to a place of curiosity and self-exploration. They instead erect a huge, red stop sign in the middle of the coaching conversation.

- Why do you think that way?
- Why did you do that?
- Why are you talking about this topic?

Coaches may also want to avoid *how* questions. *How* implies analysis and technique. *How* prompts people to think about means rather than ends, about analysis rather than values or purposes. A *how* question typically sends listeners into their heads.

Catalytic questions usually begin with the word *what*. W*hat* question creates a certain spaciousness that invites curiosity and exploration. It encourages reflection and investigation rather than defensiveness and self-justification.

- What would you do differently?
- What does God want?
- What is the truth you know?
- What will you do next?

With a little thought, most *why* and *how* questions can be converted into *what* questions. This small amount of effort can yield big dividends in the coaching conversation.

Catalytic Questions are Open-Ended

A good coaching question is open-ended. Clients cannot answer it with a simple *yes* or *no* response. Questions that have a *yes* or *no* answer seldom generate higher-order thinking or deep reflection. They do not move the conversation forward. Questions that have a *yes* or *no* answer may work great in a courtroom; but they are deadly in a coaching session. Courtroom attorneys use closed-ended questions to control the direction of the conversation or to lead a witness down a certain path. Coaching is not about controlling or directing, however. It is about creativity, curiosity, and learning.

Catalytic Questions are Brief

In my classroom teaching, I have learned that the longer the question, the more likely it will sputter and fizzle out. Brief questions, on the other hand, usually rocket the discussion forward.

People typically have one of three purposes in mind when they ask long, complex questions. They may be giving hints about what the correct response should be if the listener just follows the logic of the question. Second, they are covertly giving advice in the guise of a question. The longer the question, the more coaches may inadvertently color the client's response with their own opinions. Third, they may be trying to impress the listener with their knowledge and expertise. One way to ensure that power and control remain with the client is for the coach to ask brief questions that do not try to "lead the witness" or impress the client with the coach's expertise.

The ideal question is no more than five to seven words long. At one point, I worried that such a short question would leave too much ambiguity. The hearer would not know what I was asking. Over time, I have discovered that if the question is ambiguous or confusing, the client will ask for clarification.

- What is missing?
- What are the gaps?
- What did you learn?
- What name would you give this path?

Avoid Double-Barreled Questions

Another reason to avoid long questions is to reduce the probability that you will ask a double-barreled question. Some people can be asking two different questions in one sentence: *What did your boss say and what did you get out of it?* Double-barreled questions confuse clients. They wonder which question the coach wants answered first. The more confusing the question, the less likely it will land powerfully with the client. Double-barreled questions do not prompt crisp, clear reflection. They create fuzziness and confusion.

Ask Your Question and Wait

Beginning with kindergarten, school experiences have taught people (a) most questions have one right answer; (b) teachers already know the right answer; and (c) teachers will tell us the right answer if we are silent long enough. So people have learned to keep silent in the presence of a question. If they say nothing, the speaker will eventually tell them the right answer. Why should anyone risk giving the wrong answer when everybody knows teachers will eventually announce the right one? People concluded long ago that questions are not really asked to stimulate their best thinking but as opportunities for experts to pass judgment on their inadequacies.

So coaches often ask their clients questions; and silence follows. Clients assume (a) there is one right answer; (b) the coach has it; and (c) the coach will tell them the answer if they wait long enough. Coaches need great discipline if they are not to yield to this deeply ingrained habit. Coaches, like everyone else, are also uncomfortable with silence. They are tempted to take control of the silence by answering their own question. They thus confirm their clients' unspoken belief that, if they wait long enough, the "expert" will give the right answer; and they will not embarrass themselves by having blurted out something inadequate or wrong.

Coaches may also yield to another temptation. They interpret the client's silence as misunderstanding or confusion. So they repeat the question. But, even when they think they are asking the same question, they seldom state it with precisely the same words. They inadvertently change the wording. Sometimes this change is very slight. In other cases, they actually ask a totally different question. In either case, clients are confused. Which question should they answer: The first one or the second one? Clients will usually sink into silence out of confusion and uncertainty.

The best response, when a question is greeted by silence, is to say nothing and simply wait. I often ask a question and then count silently to fifteen so I am not tempted to answer my own question in the silence that follows it. Remember, clients are also uncomfortable in the silence. If you as coach can wait long enough, they may decide to speak just to break the silence. If they do not speak, ask them to rephrase what they thought you were asking. Or ask them what they believe the silence means. Whatever you do, do not rephrase the question yourself.

If you tape record yourself in a coaching session or Sunday school class, you will probably be surprised by how often you ask a different question when you think you are posing the same question twice. Coaches and teachers can immediately improve their questioning skills just by changing this one, high-leverage behavior.

Reflective Inquiry

One special kind of question is a reflective inquiry (Whitworth, Kimsey-House, & Sandahl 1998, pp 73-75). It shares many of the same qualities as a catalytic question, only it is not meant to be answered quickly but explored over time. It resists a quick, spur-of-the-moment answer. A good reflective inquiry demands in-depth thought over an extended period. This reflective quality is what differentiates a good question from an inquiry. Inquiries open up the possibility of introspection, meditation, and contemplation over time.

- What does it mean for you to become the Gospel for those around you?
- Where do you most resist God?
- What has become an idol?
- Where does grace live in you?
- Where do your gifts meet the world's needs?

Coaches typically pose a reflective inquiry at the end of a coaching session. The reflective inquiry is the client's homework assignment between appointments.

Figure 6.2 Characteristics of Catalytic Questions

Type of Question	Characteristics	Examples
Value-Neutral	Avoid making statements or giving advice in the form of a question	Not : *Do you actually think a youth director would improve your ministry?* Instead: *What about a youth minister would change your congregation's life?*
Positive	Point to the future, not the past Ask what is next rather than requesting explanations of what happened before	Not: *How did things get to such a point in the choir?* Instead: *What can you do to address the choir's lack of collaboration?*
Ask *What,* Not *Why*	*Why* questions create defensiveness and self-justification. *How* questions invite analysis *What* questions create space	Not: *Why did you do that?* Not: *How did you do that?* Instead: *What led you to do what you did?*
Open-Ended	Cannot be answered with a "yes" or "no" response	Not: *Are you talking to Bob?* Instead: *What was your last conversation with Bob like?*
Brief	Are only five to seven words long	Not: *Since you have six years experience and because you have been at the church for the past three years while the council was deciding what to do about the leaky roof, which church records say has been a problem since the building was built in 1910, what do you wish you could say—if you could say it—to the Trustees chairperson?* Instead: *What do you want say to the Chairperson?*
Not Double-Barreled	Do not ask two questions at once	Not: *How did your conversation go and what are you going to do next?* Instead: *What happened in your conversation?*
Wait for An Answer	Do not re-state the question and change the wording Allow silence for the client to respond	Do not ask a question, then immediately re-phrase it if the client does not respond. Ask your question and wait. If you need to break silence first, say, *What about my question is making it difficult to answer?*

Because clients live with a reflective inquiry between coaching sessions, it deepens their learning and action over time. Coaches might ask clients to post the inquiry on their desk or by their telephone. Then, every time they see it, they are to identify another answer or angle of vision on it. Coaches might ask their clients to take 15 minutes each day and write about their inquiry in a journal. The goal is for the client to probe as many levels and dimensions of the question as possible.

Since the reflective inquiry is meant to maintain momentum around a particular issue or topic between coaching appointments, coaches may ask clients to email or fax them every day with a summary of their inquiry. I once worked with a client who liked to write haiku poetry. Her homework was to spend time with the reflective inquiry and each evening email me a haiku that summarized her thoughts.

If you give someone a reflective inquiry as homework, be sure to ask about the fruit of the client's introspection at the next coaching appointment. To give an inquiry and then never discuss it will communicate only one thing: You are not really interested in the client's accountability for action or learning.

Telling the Truth

Skillful listening also involves telling the truth. Coaches are listening for the gaps between what clients say they want and what they are actually doing. Most people glide over this discrepancy. They avoid being truthful with themselves. When coaches hear these gaps, they name them and invite clients to explore them. They tell the truth. They name what clients have elsewhere in their lives made undiscussible. Human beings have an amazing capacity for remaining unaware of uncomfortable realities. They need at least one place where they can tell the truth and take responsibility for living authentically. For many people, the coaching alliance can be such a place of truth, transparency, and authenticity.

Human beings will go to great extremes to evade facing unpleasant truths. When people act to save face, they distort reality. They make negative attributions about other people or institutions, deflecting blame from themselves to outside forces. They draw illogical and unsupportable conclusions. They pretend not to know things they really do know. Or they pretend to know things about which they are genuinely ignorant. They cover up mistakes and then hide the fact that they have covered them up. As a result, they get bogged down by their own denial and evasion of the truth.

These behaviors are what Chris Argyris (1993, pp. 49-66) calls "defensive routines." Defensive routines allow people to push uncomfortable truths and unpleasant facts out of their awareness. Unfortunately, when people use defensive routines to suppress difficult truths, they make it impossible to correct the underlying causes of their embarrassment and fear.

A defensive routine is therefore self-reinforcing. It is a combination of wishful thinking and anticipatory face-saving. So long as we render things that are embarrassing or threatening undiscussible, we don't have to take responsibility for doing anything about them. And the longer we do nothing about them, the more often they will happen. And their stubborn refusal to disappear only increases our need to pretend we do not know they are happening.

So people ignore failures or exaggerate them. They avoid seeing the whole picture, allowing their mental map of a situation to remain vague, scattered, and ambiguous. They never surface and test their assumptions. So long as people remain mired down in their defensive routines, they usually make matters worse when they try to address issues created by their own behavior. A church leader wants more involvement and so talks to members in ways that shame them, thus further undermining cooperation rather than gaining it. A lay leader tries to solve a conflict by determining who is to blame, which only deepens the polarization.

Genuine learning and change occur when peoplee stop engaging in defensive routines. They stop tolerating their scattered perceptions and vague mental maps. They refuse to live any longer with ambiguous analyses of what is happening. They no longer make unilateral attributions that the source of their problems is somewhere "out there." They stop ignoring the gaps or incongruities between what they say and what they do.

The coaching relationship offers a safe, trustworthy, and truthful space where clients can confront their defensive routines and tell the truth to themselves. Coaches listen skillfully for times when clients are acting to save face, covering up, or drawing illogical conclusions. They ask clients to tell the truth about their lives

Coaches help people find the courage to explore the unintended consequences of their own behavior. Most people act in ways that are logical within their assumptive frameworks and unexamined mental models. But they do not check out these assumptions. They do not submit them to a reality test to see whether these are just groundless rules they have made up or how things really are. They fail to see the unintended consequences of what they do. For the things people usually do to avoid embarrassment or threat typically do not really eliminate the source of their embarrassment or threat. They may experience some short-term relief. But, in the long run, their denial renders them more bound and blinded by their anxieties.

Effective coaches do not let people step over these undiscussibles and defensive routines. When they ask questions that invite clients to look at incongruities and gaps, coaches need to avoid being judgmental. They are not engaged in a game of "Gotcha!" Coaches can learn to say what they mean without being mean-spirited. They are not looking for opportunities to lecture, teach, or correct. They are listening for discrepancies, vagueness, and gaps. When they hear such a discrepancy or gap, they simultaneously invite and challenge clients to tell the truth.

By telling the truth about these gaps, coaches help clients learn to challenge their assumptions and re-design their actions. Coaches cannot do this work for clients. But, by asking the right questions, they can challenge people to act courageously and tell the truth about their lives.

- What part have you contributed to this situation?
- What really scares you?
- What are you tolerating that you shouldn't be?
- What unspoken assumption are you making?
- What are you unwilling to change?
- What are you refusing to see?
- What do you know but won't admit?
- What are you going to have to give up?
- What would someone else say about this if you asked them for advice?
- What is another conclusion you could draw?
- What is your evidence?
- What has always served you before that may not be working for you now?

Building Momentum Through Action

Once people finally tell the truth, they no longer stay mired down in old routines. They are empowered to risk acting in new ways. Getting people into action is crucial because coaching is ultimately about action, outcomes, and results.

Clients may act in a way that violates a previously unspoken assumption just to see what happens. They may want to test out different behaviors just to observe how they and others react. They may talk about something that was previously an undiscussible. A coach might, for example, suggest that a client who has always assumed "no one will like me if I say 'no'" to say "no" to 50 people before the next appointment. If clients admit they are afraid of making mistakes and therefore hide and cover up their mistakes, coaches might propose they deliberately try to make 100 mistakes before the next session and tell someone about them just to see what really happens.

In addition to accountability, which we have previously discussed, coaches use three other skills to build momentum for change through concrete actions: Asking permission, requesting, and challenging.

Asking Permission

Either during the intake session or in another early session, coaches need to explain what asking permission means in the coaching alliance. This relationship exists solely for the client and the client's agenda. The client is always in control of the relationship and responsible for it. Therefore, if coaches wish to explore a sensitive area or an embarrassing topic, they ask permission before going there. Clients then have the responsibility for saying whether they want this discussion or not. The coach must be prepared, if the client says "no," to respect the client's wishes.

With practice and experience, coaches know when to ask permission and when to pursue an issue without permission. Asking permission is especially important if the coach wishes to offer specific advice or give feedback. For example, the coach might say, "Would you like some feedback on how I experience your behavior?" The client, then, can say either

- "Yes, I would like some feedback,"
- "No, I do not want feedback," or,
- "I would like feedback but not right now. Can we negotiate another time to discuss this?"

Making Requests

Coaches sometimes have a little more perspective on a client's situation and may believe a particular action could produce significant learning or be a leverage point for improved performance. In these circumstances, coaches may choose to give input rather than draw information or possibilities from the client. Coaches may request that clients commit themselves to taking some proposed action. (Whitworth, Kimsey-House, & Sandahl 1998, pp. 88-89) If a Christian educator has been struggling with recruiting Sunday school teachers, for example, her coach might request she draw up a list of ten potential volunteers before the next appointment.

The challenge in making such a request is to do so without taking real freedom of choice away from the client. To propose or request an action is not the same as imposing it upon the client. Whenever a coach makes a request for specific actions, the goal always remains the same: To permit clients to better understand themselves and their situations.

Before making a request, coaches need to see if their proposal passes three tests:

- What is my intention in making this request? Am I attached to it?

- Will it leave responsibility and freedom of choice with the client?
- Will it foster genuine action and learning?

Coaches do not make requests just to have clients doing something. They make requests so that clients can learn, grow, and discover their own power of choice. These three questions are inter-related. If coaches are genuinely committed to their clients' learning, they will not be attached to any particular proposal they make. And, when they are not attached, they are less likely to pressure clients into accepting their requests.

If coaches make a request, they must not be attached to it. If the coach is attached to a particular result or outcome, then it is the coach's agenda and not the client's. Coaches can easily be hooked by the cleverness of their own suggestions or by believing that because an idea once worked for them it will work for someone else. Part of creating safety and trust is detachment from particular outcomes.

When David came to Saul and offered to fight Goliath, he believed David was too small and inexperienced. So before sending David forth to battle, Saul clothed David with his own armor and put his bronze helmet on his head and placed his coat of mail over him. Saul then gave David his own sword. When David tried to walk, he felt loaded down and awkward. So he said to Saul, "I cannot walk with these; for I am not used to them." (1 Sam 17:39) David then removed Saul's battle gear. He took his staff and sling, found five smooth stones in the wadi, and faced Goliath on the battlefield. He did not kill Goliath with Saul's armor. He defeated him using weapons that worked for him.

Like Saul, coaches can become attached to certain outcomes, results, or ideas. They want to load down their clients with these suggestions or activities. But these proposed actions are like Saul putting his own armor on David. Rather than strengthening David for combat, Saul's battle gear simply weighed him down. It did not fit who David was or what he wanted to do. If coaches are making a request, they cannot be attached to their own proposal. The coaching alliance is about the client and what he or she needs in order to move forward. It is not about the coach's agenda or favorite strategies.

Requests have a particular phrasing and sequence. (See Figure 6.3) A request is specific and measurable. The client's accountability for it can be specified and measured. A request also asks clients to commit to whatever action they agree to do. A coach might say, "I am requesting that you find five tasks this week that you will delegate to someone else on your church staff. Will you do that?" Or, "I am requesting that you identify five continuing education opportunities happening in the next six months that focus on youth ministry, including topics, dates, locations, and costs. Will you do that?"

Clients always have three choices when responding to a request. In orienting clients to coaching tools, coaches need to talk about the client's options when receiving a request. These responses are acceptance, refusal, or counter-offer:

- "Yes. I will identify five continuing education opportunities,"
- "No. I do not feel I can do that," or,
- "I would like to make a counter-offer. I don't think I can identify five opportunities. But I will commit to finding three."

If the response is "yes," clients then need to describe their accountability. What will they do? When will they do it? And how will the coach know the client has taken action? If the client's response is "no," coaches may explore the client's reasoning. They may even explain their rationale for making the original request. The coach may not, however, pressure the client. Choice always belongs with the client.

When clients refuse a request, then the coach asks what they will do instead. The objective is not the specific action proposed by the coach. The objective is getting clients moving so they learn or do something more than what has been happening. For this reason, coaches need to be clear that the action they propose actually will move the client farther into action and learning. Some schools load up their students with worksheets and homework. The student is feverishly completing worksheets; but are they learning? In the same way, coaches need to make sure they are not making requests just so the client has something to do. The request ought to move forward the client's agenda.

Making a Challenge

A challenge is like a request, only it goes beyond the client's comfort level. Most clients have self-imposed limits as to what they think is possible for them. A good challenge asks clients to take actions that go beyond these self-imposed limits (Downey 2003, pp. 88-89). A coach knows they have issued a challenge when the client gasps or exclaims, "I can't possibly do that!"

An authentic challenge arises from the coach's belief in the client's potential capacities and abilities. Coaches may believe more in clients than that they believe in themselves. The challenge is an attempt to awaken clients to how they are performing below their potential.

The format for making a challenge is the same as for making a request: (See Figure 6.3) The coach suggests a specific, measurable goal and asks for commitment. "I challenge you to take one hour every day and do absolutely nothing—don't read, don't work on lists, don't listen to music. Just do absolutely nothing for one hour every day. Will you commit yourself to that?"

Clients usually respond to a challenge by making a counter-offer. "I can't do absolutely nothing for a whole hour every day. How about ten minutes?" The coach might press back, "You can do more than ten minutes. How about twenty minutes every day? Will you make a commitment to twenty minutes daily?"

Clients then describe their accountability for any challenge to which they commit themselves. What will they do? When will they do it? And how will the coach know the client has taken action?

Whether the client commits to ten or twenty minutes is not the point. The real objective is to get clients doing something beyond their previously self-imposed

Figure 6.3 Format For Requests And Challenges

State specific, measurable action

⇩

Ask for commitment

⇩

Client accepts
Client rejects
Client makes counter-offer

⇩

Coach and Client Agree Upon
Accountability

limits. If a church planter has said she is so busy that she does not have time to relax, just getting her to take ten minutes a day for herself is substantially more than she has been doing. A good challenge will move people outside their comfort zones. Like the request, a challenge serves as a catalyst for high-leverage action and new learning.

CHAPTER SEVEN

COACH AS COMPASS

Compasses orient people to where they are and which direction they want to go. But they do not determine the road people must travel. They set a general direction, not a specific path. In the same way, coaches orient people to where they are and where they want to go. But coaches, like compasses, never determine the path. They allow clients the flexibility and freedom to choose their own goals and plan their own futures.

Coaching focuses on results. People come to coaching because they feel stuck and want to get different results. One of the primary ways that coaches help people get different results is by serving as compasses. They walk alongside clients as they orient themselves to where they currently are, define the direction they want to go, and build bridges between the present and the future.

To get different results, people often need a different compass and a more accurate map. Coaches encourage clients to look critically at the current maps that guide their journeys. They remind them that the map is not the territory, challenging them to spin their compasses so they can see from new angles of vision. Once clients have re-oriented themselves to different perspectives, coaches walk alongside them as they plan and set new goals. They champion and acknowledge them as they make progress.

This compass-like process of orienting and pointing includes some specific strategies and tools. (See Figure 1.7) This chapter will explore these components of a coach's toolkit.

Figure 7.1 Compass Points to New Results

Identify Client's Current Mental Map

Explore Alternative Maps

Gain Commitment to a New Map

Establish New Vision As Compass for Results

Develop Goals and Action Plans

Create Structures to Support Goals and Plans

Deal with Inner Resistance to Change

Champion and Acknowledge Client

Gaining New Angles of Vision

A friend of mine teaches painting. He and other painters use a spot screen card to help determine an object's true color. One day my friend asked me what color a certain object in the distance really was. "It's blue-green ," I replied. He then handed me a card with a small hole in it. "Now look at the same object through the hole," he said. Holding the card to my eye, I realized it was not blue-green at all. When I isolated it from its context, it looked different from what I had assumed.

Everyone has some contextual frame that makes it difficult to see the world as it really is. People develop assumptions about "the way things are" as a mental convenience. When they assume something is true, they no longer have to spend time looking carefully at reality. Unfortunately, what people assume to be true often prevents them from seeing new possibilities.

The first three compass points for getting new results in people's lives are (a) helping them realize they are stuck in a narrow perspective, (b) exploring alternative maps of their situation, and (c) gaining commitment to a new perspective from which they can create a vision of God desired future for them.

Assumptive Frames as a Shortcut to Reality

People's frames are a shortcut used to simplify reality. Human beings must exclude large chunks of sensory data in order to reduce the world to workable proportions. Frames make it easier to deal with complex situations or large amounts of incoming information. Unfortunately, people sometimes need this excluded information to solve problems or respond creatively to new challenges.

Just as a building takes shape around its basic architectural frame—contractors even speak of "framing" a house—so a point of view takes shape around whatever frame within which it is conceived and presented. Once a building is framed, you cannot just put a door or window anywhere. The building's basic frame, once erected, shapes what is and is not possible. We shape our buildings and then our buildings shape us. Mental frames similarly both define and limit a person's thinking. They enhance a prevailing viewpoint and restrict awareness of competing information.

People soon treat their assumptions as facts and let these assumptive frameworks shape the decisions they make, the commitments they honor, and the goals they believe possible. People do all this without much thought as to whether or not their assumptive frames accurately represent the whole of reality. They have no equivalent of a painter's spot screen card to test out their assumed truths.

Just as a picture frame puts a boundary on an image and, through its shape, texture, or color, draws the eye's attention to some aspects of the painting and not to others, so people's mental frames put boundaries on their imaginations and draw their thoughts to some aspects of a situation but not to others. These assumptive frames determine people's beliefs about themselves and what they can or cannot do. Frames affect how people see their role in life. They limit what people think is possible.

The metaphors people use in everyday conversation reveal how they are unconsciously aware of this phenomenon. People describe someone as having "tunnel vision," meaning they see events or people from only a single, usually narrow, perspective. Individuals say they were "blindsided" by events, meaning they had a limited perspective that prevented them from seeing other factors that ultimately proved important.

Simply changing a frame or perspective dramatically influences what people believe they can or cannot do. If someone tells us that we have one month to complete a task, our response will likely be very different than if they tell us that we have one year. Simply changing the time perspective alters our emotional response as well as our actual behavior. This process of changing one's perspective or assumptive framework is called re-framing. The purpose of re-framing is to help people experience their beliefs, actions, and values from different perspectives so they can have more flexibility and power of choice about what they do.

Re-Framing and Coaching

Re-framing is a key strategy for effective coaching. Coaches help clients identify their assumptive frameworks and then explore how the same situation looks when viewed through different perspectives.

Re-framing is actually a very common activity. Most jokes rely on some type of re-framing. The punch line forces hearer to re-frame their expectations, which produces surprise and humor. Politicians use re-framing all the time. When Ronald Reagan met Walter Mondale in the 1984 presidential debates, the media were discussing Reagan's age as a factor in the election. During one debate, Reagan turned the issue around by promising not to make an issue of Mondale's youth and inexperience. Movies like *It's A Wonderful Life* or novels like *A Christmas Carol* depend on re-framing. The main characters re-think the meaning of their lives after seeing themselves from different perspectives.

People come to coaching because they feel stuck or bogged down in their lives. In fact, they are bogged down or stuck in a narrow perspective that has limited their ability to perceive other options and possibilities. It has hindered them from recognizing their own power and creativity. When people are stuck in one assumptive framework or perspective, they need an environment that simultaneously challenges and supports them as they look critically at their mental models of reality, recognize alternative points-of-view, and realize they have the power and freedom to choose other possibilities.

Our perspective on an event radically shapes both our emotional response and our actions. For example, when the electricity goes out in my office, I can view it as a major inconvenience. My computer will not work. The air conditioning shuts down. I cannot get the copier to work. I feel angry, frustrated, depressed. I pace the floor and complain to others around me. Or I can reframe the power outage as a gift. I relax or go home to play with my children. What I do and how I feel are not determined by forces outside myself. I determine how I feel and act by the power of my own thoughts. Through our thinking, we create the world around us; and then we say, "I did not do this. It was done to me."

Human beings are quite frequently held captive by their own patterns of thought. When people limit the meaning of a situation to one, narrow perspective—which may not even accurately reflect reality—they limit their resources and their possibilities. Through skillful listening and catalytic questions, coaches help clients re-frame their experiences and explore other possible meanings they can give to situations.

One way to encourage clients to examine situations from different perspectives is to create a reframing matrix (Senge, et al 1994, pp.273-275). The situation is written in the center box. Then, in the first section around this central box, clients describe their current viewpoint using a brief phrase or word. Then, in the remaining sections, they brainstorm other possible perspectives using a short phrase or word. (See Figure 7.2) It is important to help clients identify at least seven or eight different possible frames-of-reference for this situation. Usually the first two or three alternatives offered by the client are really just different ways of re-stating his or her original perspective.

Hunting for our most deeply held assumptive frameworks is hard work. We have typically invested a great deal of time and effort in constructing the perspectives that guide our lives. Parting with these comfortable and familiar points of view is never easy.

In Matthew's gospel, Jesus tells a parable about a merchant who finds a pearl of great price. (Matt 13:45-46) Then he goes and sells everything he has to possess this one pearl. Jesus says the kingdom of heaven is like the merchant. Whatever else Jesus is trying to say, he is surely suggesting that the kingdom of heaven is not something immediately presented to us on a silver platter and all we have to do is put it in our wallet or purse and go home. To gain the kingdom of heaven we have to give up something else of great value to us. We have to make a new choice about what matters most, about how we will see our selves, our world, and our God. To choose a new, Spirit-shaped perspective, we have to be willing to part with the other, lesser pearls that have guided our thinking and acting.

Once at least seven or eight alternative viewpoints are identified, client and coach can discuss how the situation or goal looks and feels from each one. This process should not be completely cerebral and logical. Clients need to recognize how different assumptive models make them feel, not just what they rationally suggest:

- What would you expect to happen if you look at your situation from this perspective?
- What would you expect never to happen if you look at your situation from this perspective?
- What does time look like? Is there more time or less to get things done?
- Does this situation seem more urgent or less urgent when looked at from this viewpoint?
- What resources appear or disappear when you look at things from this viewpoint?
- What or who does this perspective let you see, which would otherwise remain hidden?
- What or who does this perspective make it difficult for you to see?
- Which frame would you really like to see the world from?
- What frame of reference would you choose if you were all God wanted you to be?

This discussion allows clients to realize they have choices about how they view themselves and their situations. When people have become stuck and are not getting the results they want, they have usually become locked into a very narrow viewpoint that blinds them to other options, resources, and opportunities. When people are both blinded by and bound to one narrow perspective, they forget they have the freedom to choose. They make themselves passive victims of their assumptions. In the past they may have made a choice to internalize a certain point-of-view. They have the same freedom to make a different choice now.

The goals of this exercise are to (a) free the client from the grip their current assumptive framework or mental model; (b) encourage them to imagine alternative mental maps and evaluate how their situation looks from these other perspectives; (c) realize they have the power to choose the frame through which they will see themselves and their world; and (d) commit themselves to a new map from which they want to create a vision of the future.

This process is not simply "sugar-coating" a bad situation by calling it an opportunity. It involves genuinely seeing the situation from another perspective and making a choice that serves one's life purposes better. The last step in this compass point for new results is asking clients to make a commitment to create a new vision of God's purposes for their lives from this place rather than from their old perspective.

Figure 7.2   Reframing Matrix

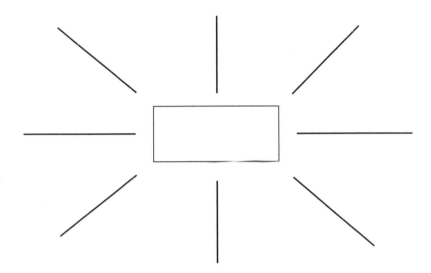

Establishing New Compass Points for Results

Re-framing reminds clients they have the power to choose how they see the world. They can see it from their limited perspective. Or they can stretch their vision and see at least a little more of how the world must look from God's point-of-view. Once people have broken free from the narrow perspectives that bind and blind them, they can commit themselves to a more powerful vision of their future. Without this new place from which to create a clearer vision of where God is calling them, people will create a predictable future rather than a creative future. They will envision the future merely as an extension of the past rather than as something genuinely new and creative.

When people want to construct a predictable future, they are usually focusing on their problems and not their choices. They are still attached to the previous mental assumptions that have limited their thinking and acting. Without being able to frame and re-frame their assumptive frameworks, clients will likely set future goals based on their old perspectives of what is or is not possible. But the future does not have to be an extension of the past. It can be something entirely different.

Christians, of all people, should believe transformation is possible. Scripture consistently and persistently invites people to transformation and change. When Christians deny people can have futures different from their past, they deny the power of the resurrection. What is the call to repent if not an invitation to change and transformation? The Bible consistently reminds Christians that their God is one who creates hopeful futures, not predictable ones. "Do not remember the former things, or consider the things of old. I am about to do a new thing; now it springs forth, do you not perceive it?" (Isa 43:18-19)

As people identify their assumptive frameworks and limited perspectives, they discover they have the power to choose how they look at themselves and their world. Their viewpoints are not fixed and frozen but fluid and dynamic. Having chosen to see things in one way at a previous point does not mean they have surrendered their freedom of choice for all time.

Coaches help client declare what they are passionate about and what they honestly believe God has given them the potential to create. They invite clients to stand inside this envisioned future and create from it.

Powerful visions for the future share several common characteristics. First, they do not come just from our own thoughts and desires. They come from beyond us. Visions are ultimately a matter of inspiration. Inspiration literally means "to breathe in the Spirit." Moses did not just sit down after a hard day following his father-in-law's sheep around the desert and say, "I think I will go back to Egypt and free my people." Moses' vision came from beyond himself. It came from God. Paul did not sit down, draw up a list of the advantages and disadvantages of Christianity, and then decide rationally that he would become a missionary to the Gentiles. A vision on the Damascus Road came unannounced and unexpectedly.

Second, visions are clear and specific. They are not abstract ideas. A vision's capacity to motivate arises from its specificity. People actually see the picture created by the vision. Visions need to be clear enough that people will recognize the results when they see them. A vision's clarity and specificity are important because a visual picture assimilates a large amount of information all at once. A picture, we say, is worth a thousand words. A visually clear picture of the future to which God is calling us can give information that cannot be conveyed in another way. This is one reason clients always find it easier to construct a predictable future rather than a desired future. It is much easier to build a future that looks like the past than something totally new.

Coaches help their clients paint clear, specific, and visually detailed pictures of the future. What will they be doing on their ideal day? What are some of the people they will interact with? Where will they work and what will that environment feel or look like? Some coaches might ask their clients to journal about their vision. Others might suggest clients draw an actual picture of what their future looks like. Still others might use guided meditations to transport their clients into God's future. The clearer the client's visual picture, the more easily clients can move toward it and recognize it when they achieve it.

Third, visions are not about solving problems. They are about creating something new. A vision is not the same thing as a solution. A vision is what people genuinely want to move toward, not what they are desperately fleeing from. A huge chasm separates the questions, "What is the problem and how do we fix it?" from, "What is the future we want to create?" Coaches need to be alert to when clients are creating a possible future and when they are merely finding solutions to unpleasant difficulties.

Setting Goals

Goals are the action steps that move clients toward their envisioned future. A useful goal can be expressed in an action statement that is specific, measurable, achievable, rewarding, and timely. The acronym SMART is sometimes used for such goals

S   specific

M   measurable

A   achievable

R   rewarding

T   timely or time-specific

Goals that are specific can be pictured clearly in the client's mind. He or she can state it succinctly and powerfully. When a goal is measurable, clients can gauge their progress toward it and have criteria for knowing when they have achieved it. Feeling one's movement toward a goal that is measurable can powerfully motivate an individual when their interest or energy otherwise might begin to dissipate.

Achievable goals are realistic. Some people set goals that are too easy. Others establish unrealistically high goals. Neither motivates people. Easy goals fail to inspire people's best efforts. Goals that are far beyond someone's capabilities result in frustration and despair. A goal that is too easy suggests an individual may have a strong fear of failure. Setting an easily attained goal feels safer, even if it does not really move the client toward their vision. Coaches play a critical role in helping clients identify goals that have enough challenge to stretch their abilities but are not so difficult that clients despair and give up.

Goals are rewarding when clients can easily tie their goal-oriented actions back into their vision. If clients cannot see how a goal moves them toward their vision, they have little reason to pursue it actively and energetically. A goal that is clearly related to the client's envisioned future will sustain momentum even through the difficult times.

Finally, goals should have a specified timeline. Time is part of the price paid for the reward of achieving a goal. People need to understand from the very outset that some goals will take longer than others. In fact, coaches might encourage clients to establish a number of different timeframes for their goals. Some goals might be short-term; others, medium- and long-term. This mix of different timelines can encourage clients to have a long-term perspective as well as receive some immediate feedback that can motivate them to continue. Time-based deadlines help protect clients from both procrastination and perfectionism.

SMART goals constitute the client's roadmap to his or her vision.

- What are the SMART action steps that you will take toward your vision?
- How will you measure your progress?
- When will you do next?

An effective goal will not just be SMART. It will answer the "five W's"—*who, what, when, where,* and *how.* Goals that answer these questions can define priorities and establish direction. They motivate and inspire.

Coaches can also encourage clients to set goals that are positively stated. Most goals are better stated as positive outcomes. For example, a client might want to set as their goal: *To have no classes without teachers the first Sunday of September.* The coach might work with the client to state this as a positive goal: *To have a teacher for every class by the first Sunday in September.*

Coaches also need to guide clients toward setting goals that are performance-based rather than outcome-based. *To have a teacher for every class by the first Sunday of September* is actually an outcome. But clients cannot really control the outcomes of their activities. They can only control their own performance. A better goal might be *To contact at least three people each week between now and August 15, asking them to serve as Sunday school teachers beginning the first Sunday in September.* By answering the five W's, this goal is both performance-oriented and positive.

Creating Life Structures and Daily Practices

In order to say *yes* to one goal or purpose, people also have to say *no* to something else. The Christian understandings of both temptation and asceticism bear this simple concept within them. When we yield to temptation, we are saying a *yes* to something desirable that contains within it a *no* to God. We are so focused on our *yes* that we do not realize until too late that we have simultaneously said *no* to God. Asceticism, conversely, focuses on the things to which we must say *no* if we are to say *yes* to God. When we fast, for example, we are not saying *no* to food just for the sake of saying *no*. Our *no* is ultimately for the sake of a *yes* to God. We become empty that God might fill us. Good Christian practice entails asking both about our *yes* and our *no* in any given situation.

Coaches help clients clarify what they are saying *no* to as they say *yes* to their vision and goals. Coaches also remind clients how they are saying *no* to their vision when they continue saying *yes* to all their old habits, attitudes, and assumptions.

Most clients need help creating structures that remind them of their *yes* and their *no*. (Kegan and Lahey 2001, pp. 230-234) Most physicians will say the weakest link in medical treatment is patients' noncompliance. Physicians prescribe medicine that patients do not take. They refuse to follow treatment regimes that doctors establish. Most management consultants will say the same pattern undermines their recommendations. They give good advice; yet clients refuse to follow it. Why? They lack structures in their daily lives that remind them of the commitments they have made and the actions they need to take.

Medical treatments are more successful when patients have some sort of structure that helps them remember what they are to do. Older adults sometimes have a box with seven slots. Atop each slotted compartment is a day of the week. The pills for that day are placed in each compartment so they know what days they take which pills. This box is a structure. It reminds someone of the treatment regime to which they have committed themselves.

People usually do not lack commitment to self-chosen goals. But they may need help sustaining that commitment over time. Sustaining commitment requires supporting structures that remind and hold accountable. An intimate connection exists between the practices and habits that structure our daily lives and the values or purposes we hold. Wall Street marketers understand this relationship much better than the church. Marketing firms study how people's values express themselves in purchasing choices and patterns of consumption. Advertisements are carefully tailored to reflect the values and life purposes of certain market segments. "If you purchase this product," they promise, "you can have the life you desire for yourself." Concrete habits and life structures—like what toothpaste we purchase—are closely linked to values and attitudes we hold.

Church organizations sometimes purchase this same marketing research. They use it to determine where to locate a new congregation or what programs a church should embrace to reach its community. They fail to see the deeper implications of this research. Our vision and values are embodied in very practical structures and daily habits.

Moving toward an envisioned future is not just a matter of painting a clear picture and setting SMART goals. Realizing this new future also depends on grounding it in specific life structures and daily habits. Coaches help clients create structures that embody their vision.

The coaching practice of accountability is one such structure. It requires discipline. It creates focus. It sustains commitment. As they walk alongside clients, coaches explore with them ways to create multiple, sometimes redundant structures that embed action steps toward their desired future into concrete, here-and-now practices. These structures prompt clients into the actions to which they have committed themselves.

For example, one pastor's goal was to increase the amount of exercise she got each week. With her coach's help, she created a structure that included an exercise partner. It was much easier for her to get up an hour early three weekday mornings to swim at 6 A.M. if she knew her neighbor would be meeting her at the pool. To turn off the alarm and go back to sleep was not a possibility when someone else was waiting for her.

Calendars, planners, and to-do lists are structures. People can write certain events or activities into their calendars, thus reminding themselves of the actions to which they have committed themselves. Having set a definite appointment in one's calendar also keeps other events and activities from crowding out important commitments to action. One Christian educator found it easier to keep the discipline of daily prayer when it was scheduled into her planner and placed on her to-do list. Otherwise, she found it too easy to let other activities take precedence over it

Coaches and clients can become creative and imaginative in creating structures that support the client's goal-focused behavior. One person might tape messages to his telephone or calendar. One pastor, for instance, taped a brief statement of her life purpose to the front of her planning calendar. She sees the statement every time she opens her calendar. It reminds her to judge whatever she is about to schedule against this purpose. Someone else put a rubber band around his wrist and snapped it every time he repeated an old message about himself that he knew was getting in the way of moving toward his envisioned future. Another bought a stuffed toy that looked like a monster. He put it on the corner of his desk. Every time one of his old self-limiting thoughts seemed to be taking over, he looked at the stuffed animal and remembered these thoughts had no more power than a stuffed toy. This simple act broke the old pattern's hold over him

Dealing with Resistance

About six weeks into the coaching alliance, as clients begin to make significant progress toward their goals and purposes, they usually encounter a time of resistance. This resistance may take many forms. They may lose interest and energy. They may encounter setbacks and fall into old habits and practices. They may find themselves slipping back into old assumptions and perspectives they thought they had left behind. Coaches need to help clients name and work through this period of resistance.

Resistance to change is neither good nor bad. It is simply a natural and usually unconscious process of slowing or blocking progress toward significant change. It occurs when people realize that really changing their ministries means losing things that are comfortable, familiar, and precious. People resist because they become anxious about the unknown effects of their new actions. One positive aspect of resistance is that it allows people to consolidate past gains before moving forward again. It can, however, impede growth and movement if people linger too long in it.

Signs of resistance are easy to recognize. A client may want to gather more and more information about possible actions or goals or ideas. No matter how much data they gather, they always want more before they act. Another client may flood the coach with details and stories. The more clients share, the less they actually do. Still other clients will go on the attack, questioning their coach's competency or skills. Sometimes, resistance expresses itself as confusion. They will go over the same questions or issues again and again. Both intellectualizing or moralizing about their lives can also be a form of resistance. Theorizing or moralizing about life in general can be a way to avoid actually doing anything productive and concrete about one's life.

When resistance surfaces, coaches need to remember that clients are not resisting them or even the coaching relationship. They are resisting the unknown. They are resisting losing familiar perspectives and ways of being in the world.

Resistance is an indirect expression of feelings of fear and anxiety. Since it is an emotional process, coaches cannot address it through logic or reasoning. They can only address it at the level of the client's emotions and feelings.

Coaches name how they are experiencing a client's resistance in a neutral, nonjudgmental manner. The real skill is in naming the resistance without attacking or blaming. The best way is to describe what one is observing or experiencing.

Clients will usually respond with a more direct statement of the emotions they are feeling. This expression creates an opening where the coach and client can explore the larger dynamic of resistance.

Once the resistance has been expressed, coaches can invite clients to examine why it has surfaced at this particular point.

- What are the unspoken messages they are giving themselves?
- What are they fearing might happen?
- What about this particular action or goal is especially difficult?

As clients begin to name their resistance, coaches need to offer emotional support. Since resistance is an emotional process, emotional support for addressing it plays an especially significant role.

Finally, coaches can pose questions about the future:

- What are the future implications for you if you do nothing to change what is happening now?
- If you keep on the same path you are right now, what are the consequences?

Coach and client can then identify next steps for addressing the resistance. What concretely can the client do to move forward in spite of fears, anxieties, or threats? What self-limiting judgments need acknowledged and set aside?

Facing resistance is about standing in the midst of one's greatest fears and not turning back. Most people find the courage to stand in the midst of this storm when they do not stand alone, but with a trusted companion alongside them. A coach becomes such a companion. He or she stands alongside the client amid this storm of fear, anxiety, and self-doubt. And, when they stand together facing this storm, clients discover that what they have feared the most rises up and blesses them.

Championing and Acknowledging

As clients move through their fears and take steps toward their envisioned futures, coaches play an important role as champions. When clients doubt their abilities or competencies, coaches champion them. (Whitworth, Kimsey-House, and Sandahl 1998, p. 105) They point out their clients' strengths, abilities, resourcefulness, and courage. They remind them they are capable human beings who can do much more than they imagine they can.

Years ago I lived near Boston and would sometimes join the crowds at the Boston Marathon. One year I positioned myself at Heartbreak Hill. It is near the end of the race. Runners are physically and emotionally exhausted as they approach this last uphill leg of the race. What fascinated me what how the crowd shouted and cheered for these runners. They might not personally know them, but they knew how important their encouragement was to an exhausted runner. Marathon runners often need just a little additional motivation to push them over the top. Good coaches are like the crowd at Heartbreak Hill. They walk—or perhaps run—alongside their clients and shout, "You can do it. Just a little more and you'll have made it over the top!"

Championing is not the same as giving a compliment. When coaches compliment clients, they express appreciation for what they did. "Good job on that Sunday school newsletter you started, Tonya." Championing, on the other hand, reminds the client of skills and qualities they might be inclined to overlook. "You can do this, Luis. You have all the skills and abilities to make it happen." Coaches not only challenge people to move beyond their comfort zone, they also champion their courage and resourcefulness.

An even more critical coaching skill is acknowledgement. (Hargrove 2003, pp.59-60; Belf 2002, p. 173) Acknowledgement is different than either championing or complimenting. Coaches acknowledge who someone is, not what they do. Acknowledgement recognizes someone's unique, inner attributes and values. Acknowledging clients' inner strengths validates them when they may be having trouble seeing these qualities for themselves.

Everyone needs to be acknowledged for who they are. One of our deepest human needs is to be seen and recognized not for what we do but for who we are. Acknowledgement involves recognizing who people are in all their uniqueness and giftedness as God's special creation. Being acknowledged, particularly when clients are struggling through difficult transitions, gives them the courage to know they are on the right path. Acknowledgement is a kind of compass point that reminds them of who they are and what their efforts are ultimately about.

Acknowledging someone includes both delivering the gift of acknowledgement and making sure the client has received it. Many times people want to brush off an acknowledgement. They do not want to receive messages about what values their lives exemplify. They hear the words, but do not receive the gift. Coaches need to observe how clients receive an acknowledgement. If a client is stepping over it or shrugging it off, the coach may need to pause and reinforce the gift: "Did you really let into yourself what was just shared? Don't rush on to something else. Just stop and feel the impact of what I just said to you."

Not long ago, our family went to a school event. After each act in a talent show, the audience applauded wildly. Some student performers bowed to the audience after their performance and then stood there to receive the crowd's applause.

Others lowered their heads and quickly rushed off-stage, ignoring the audience's applause. If people never let someone's appreciation, compliment, or acknowledgement land—if they never stand there and receive it fully—then they never genuinely feel their own power. They never feel the significance of what they have done. Deprived of this feeling, they impoverish their own resources. They always feel small, unable to play a bigger game. The problem, however, is not their insignificance. It is their refusal to receive the gift of acknowledgement others are giving.

Coaches have a responsibility to ensure that clients fully receive the acknowledgement, championing, and compliments that others bestow. They do not let clients lower their heads and hurry off-stage, pretending not to hear the applause.

CHAPTER EIGHT

COACH AS THINKING PARTNER

Coaching focuses on learning and performance because improvements in performance are usually triggered by significant insights and new learning. The best way to improve performance is to learn from past behavior so that future actions are more powerful, focused, and creative. Performance-oriented learning demands an honest look at the results our current actions are producing. It also requires people to examine their underlying assumptions about why they believe these actions would produce those results.

Effective coaches walk alongside their clients as thinking partners, helping them reflect on their actions and the results they are producing. Coaches use at least two skills to foster improvements in learning and performance: Meaningful feedback and reflection-in-action.

Giving Meaningful Feedback

Feedback is a powerful tool for learning. Coaches and clients cannot foster significant action, monitor progress toward goals, or assess results without feedback. Feedback that is well delivered propels a client forward. Feedback that is poorly given undermines the coaching alliance. Giving feedback may be one of the most valuable and challenging aspects of coaching.

Good feedback helps people establish the connection between their intentions and their impact. Without feedback, people are left on their own to determine what others think or feel as a result of their actions. Without feedback, people can never know how their behavior affects others. Feedback thus helps people learn something they usually cannot discover on their own. They can take a class and learn to operate a new piece of equipment. They can read a book and learn to communicate more clearly. But only through feedback can they discover what impact their actions have on others.

Good coaching does not just involve giving immediately feedback. People sometimes need help making connections between present feedback and other feedback they have received in the past. Asking for and receiving good feedback allows people to self-modulate their behavior and re-calibrate their actions so they can move toward their goals and purposes.

Feedback Is Not Advice

Feedback is not the same thing as advice. Feedback involves telling people something they cannot discover on their own. If you ask me for feedback, I am giving you something you cannot get in any other way—my perception of your behavior. Advice, on the other hand, involves sharing something that receivers could get for themselves if they looked long enough, studied harder, or had more experience.

The challenge with giving advice is to avoid making someone feel controlled. When someone gives advice, they are describing what they would do or believe the other person should do. Advice can take responsibility away from the listener. If advice does not produce the desired results, then the receiver can always say, "I did not believe this would work in the first place. I only did it because you advised me to do it."

Under certain circumstances, coaches may decide to give specific advice to clients. When this happens, coaches ought not cloak their advice or opinion in the form of feedback. Instead, they ask, "May I give you my advice? Or "May I share my own opinion with you?" The client can then decide whether to accept the invitation or refuse it. The client is also clear the coach's comments are advice or opinion. They are about the coach. They are not feedback about the client.

If the danger of advice is having the receiver feel controlled, the dilemma with feedback is making the receiver feel disempowered. Feedback reminds people of their inability to see something they otherwise could not know. Coaches need to take care in how they give feedback so clients do not feel powerless—as if they have overlooked the obvious. When someone gives feedback, they are describing the impact of the other person's behavior on them. The hearer is responsible for what he or she does with the feedback. The receiver learns something they otherwise would not know; but how they then respond is up to them.

Steps in Giving Feedback

Coaches therefore need to follow some careful steps in giving feedback to their clients. The feedback process includes at least four steps: Asking permission, giving feedback, checking for understanding, and follow-up. (See Figure 8.1)

Figure 8.1 A Process for Giving Feedback

STEP	BEHAVIORS
Asking Permission	Say: "I have some feedback to give, would you like to receive it?"
Giving Feedback	Focus on key behaviors, not secondary effects
	Focus on one or two high-leverage behaviors or actions
	Resist words that carry a judgment or imply evaluation
	Describe behavior rather than intention or motive
	Use I-language rather than you-language
	Do not cloak advice or opinion as feedback
Checking for Understanding	Ask what the client has heard. Seek clarification.
	Do not demand a response. Feedback is an observation, not a diagnosis
	Invite the client to seek feedback from others
	Invite the client to explore connections between your feedback and past feedback from others
Follow-Up	Teach or model for the client how to give and receive feedback.
	Explore with client different options for action
	Facilitate movement from feedback to action

ASKING PERMISSION

Always ask permission before giving feedback. This is the single most critical step in the feedback process. The coach begins by saying, "I have some feedback to give you, would you like to receive it?"

Asking permission helps to lower resistance. If someone asks for feedback, they are more likely to listen and follow-up. When someone receives uninvited feedback, they typically dismiss its importance, relevant, or accuracy. Asking permission also clarifies who owns the responsibility for acting on feedback. When someone asks for feedback, they accept responsibility for their own insights and follow-up actions. Thirdly, asking permission minimizes the receiver's feeling controlled or disempowered. When someone asks for feedback, they are retaining power over the conversation. Feedback is not something done to them. It is something they choose. Coaches need to respect their clients' wishes. If a client says, "No, I don't want feedback," then the coach needs to refrain from giving it.

GIVING FEEDBACK

Because it is so important to learning, coaches need to be comfortable giving feedback. If they are reluctant to share feedback, they need to examine the underlying sources of this hesitancy. The first place to look is their own attitude toward receiving feedback. If they have a negative reaction to receiving feedback, they are likely to be uncomfortable giving it.

Coaches also need to ask themselves why they are giving feedback. The coach's goal is to facilitate the client's learning. So coaches need to insure their feedback is relevant, practical, and specific. If they are frustrated or upset with a client, it is probably not a good time to give feedback. Feedback is not about changing another person's behavior. It is about sharing the impact of the client's behaviors on you. If coaches genuinely want the client to change some specific behavior, they need to say directly what they want. Do not try to change someone in the guise of giving them feedback.

Coaches also need to clarify whether the behaviors upon which they are commenting are really the key drivers of performance. People more easily give and receive feedback about secondary behaviors or actions. These appear less threatening and more easily discussed. Unfortunately, feedback about these behaviors seldom produces significant change.

Coaches also need to insure they do not give feedback on too many behaviors at once. People can typically address only one or two behaviors at any given time. If the coach floods the client with feedback on multiple behaviors and actions, then the client will probably be overwhelmed. He or she may choose to ignore the feedback. Or clients may try to address all these behaviors simultaneously and fail to make any significant changes at all.

Feedback is not the same thing as advice. But neither is it identical to constructive criticism. Criticism carries a judgment or evaluation of the other person's behavior. Coaches need to resist the temptation to evaluate or assess. To avoid this temptation, coaches can stay focused on the behavior itself or how others might experience it. "I have described your behavior's impact on me. Tell me about its impact on you," or "What could someone else see in this behavior?" Do not try to infer or guess why someone acted as they did. Find objective, nonjudgmental language to describe the behavior and its impact. Words like *lazy* or *disorganized* only give people an excuse to reject the comments. Stay with the action and its impact.

Keep feedback in the first person as much as possible. Saying things like, "You ought to . . . " or, "Other people must feel . . . " only increases the potential for resistance and denial. On the other hand, do not slip into giving advice indirectly by talking about yourself: "What worked for me when I was in a similar situation was . . ." or, "What I have found helpful is . . ."

I was once coaching the head of staff in a larger membership congregation. I had the same experience every time we met face-to-face. While we were talking, she would shuffle through papers, call to her secretary in the adjoining room about some task she had just then remembered, or engage in some other distracting behavior. I eventually asked her, "I have some feedback to give, would you like to receive it?" She said that she would. So I said, "I have come to your office several times. Both times you interrupt our conversation to tell your secretary something you have forgotten, you answer your cell phone, you turn away from me to shuffle through papers in your briefcase. When you do this, I feel like you do not value our time or me. I feel like you really do not think I am that important. When you do other things as we talk, I think you do not believe I am as smart as you are or have anything to offer that you do not already know."

She was quiet for a few moments and sat looking at me. Then she said, "My associate pastor said almost the same thing to me last week. And not long ago my son said it too."

People are generally very consistent. Their behavior does not change much across different settings. When coaches give feedback, they are typically describing a pattern that occurs elsewhere. If it shows up in the coaching relationship, it shows up in other work relationships. By pointing out this pattern and its impact, coaches help clients see their actions and results more clearly. My feedback led into a very fruitful conversation about how this pattern of distraction was undermining many relationships in her parish.

Having given feedback, coaches check to see how their clients have received it. They stop talking and listen. They ask what the client has heard or how their comments have landed.

Clients may want to put some time between feedback and their response. It is often best not to respond immediately to feedback. They may need time to reflect. They may want to seek out other feedback or to explore connections between this feedback and previous feedback they have received. Coaches might even challenge clients to seek feedback from a certain number of people before the next appointment. Coaches could also create a powerful inquiry for clients by summarizing the conversation and asking them to ponder it through the week.

Coaches may also want to ask for feedback on their feedback. By requesting feedback from their clients, coaches model how to request and receive feedback.

FOLLOW-UP ON FEEDBACK

Coaches may need to teach clients about receiving feedback. Feedback does not require an answer or response. It is an observation and not a diagnosis. Clients do not need to agree with feedback. Neither do they need to reject it or respond to it. Feedback is a gift. Like all gifts, the recipient is free to do with it as they see best. It brings with it no obligation to change a particular behavior.

Action rather than reaction is feedback's ultimate purpose. Good feedback results in action. Rather than extend a conversation about feedback, coaches and clients can move to questions of action. Does this feedback suggest a different action or behavior you could test out? What is one thing you could do differently based on this feedback?

Facilitating Reflection-in-Action

Coaches are always trying to get their clients into action. Coaching, after all, is about action, results, and outcomes. Action, however, cannot be separated from learning. All action is theory-saturated; and all theory is action-oriented. Whatever people do, they are acting on some theory or rule about cause-and-effect. These theories are usually hidden, below our conscious awareness. For people to get different results from their actions, they typically must alter these assumptive theories.

People learn in order to be safe. They convert their raw experiences into remembered meanings that serve as maps for future action. Animals are born with instincts that guide their actions. People are not. We make our way through life by learning rather than instinct. Although learning is closely tied to action, authentic learning only occurs when action is not performed unthinkingly. This dynamic constitutes the paradox of action and learning. Although our learning is for the sake of action, we can only learn when we suspend action long enough to examine our underlying mental models or assumptive theories.

Powerful actions that move people toward the outcomes they desire arise from clear, accurate, and adaptive theories-in-action. Coaches are always pressing clients into action because through action and feedback, people have a treasured opportunity. They can both learn about their unspoken perspectives on the world and make choices about how they will adapt these perspectives to get different results. Coaches encourage action because action—any action, no matter how small—leads to learning; and learning feeds forward into more powerful actions.

Mapping Our Assumptive Frameworks

Mapping is a tool that allows people to surface and reflect upon their assumptive frameworks, realize they have choices about how they look at their world, and revise the maps that guide their actions.

How Our Mental Maps Work

Our mental maps have at least six parts (Toulmin 1958, pp 97-125): (See Figure 8.1)

- Experience or information
- General beliefs
- Anticipated results
- Exceptions
- Actual results
- Emotional responses
- Decisions
- Beliefs communicated by others

Suppose the lights go out in my kitchen. (Figure 8.1 A) I have a general mental model that says when lights go out, the electrical power has been cut off to the whole house. (Figure 8.1 B) Where has this belief come from? First, it comes from prior personal experiences of power outages. (Figure 8.1 C) Second, it comes from beliefs communicated to me about power outages by friends, family, or authority figures. (Figure 8.1 D)

On the basis of my mental model, my anticipated results are that lights and clocks will be off throughout my house. (Figure 8.1 E) This evokes an emotional response of frustration because I am trying to bake a cake. Or, if I it is at night and

I live in a dangerous neighborhood, my emotional response to the power outage might be fear. (Figure 8.1 F) This creates a loop between my emotional responses and my anticipated outcomes. What I anticipate triggers certain emotions. And these emotions then shape and re-shape my anticipated results. This loop can actually short-circuit my best and most creative thinking.

But I also have some exceptions to this general model of power outages. I know that if a circuit has become overloaded in the kitchen, a breaker might be thrown. (Figure 8.1 G) In which case, the lights would be out in the kitchen but not the garage or anywhere else in the house.

So I decide to go flip the light switch in the garage to test the light whether lights are out everywhere or just in the kitchen (Figure 8.1 H) And when I go into the garage and flip the light switch, nothing happens. These actual results reinforce my general belief that power is out everywhere and no electrical appliance will run, including the oven. (Figure 8.1 I) These actual results reinforce my general mental model.

Mapping my thinking is relatively easy for a power outage in the kitchen. With additional time and thought, I can make the map more complicated and detailed.

Even looking at this relatively simple mental map, I can better understand my thinking and why I take the actions I do. My actions are based on emotional reactions, what I anticipate will happen, and my general mental map of similar situations. For example, when I check the garage light switch, I am acting on a mental assumption about possible exceptions to my general belief. Or I can see how my general mental model leads me to anticipate certain results, which prompt certain emotional responses, which then push me into certain actions.

Suppose, however, that we are not mapping a power outage in the kitchen. What if the situation were the resignation of the church's Sunday school superintendent. (Figure 8.1 A) I may have a general mental model that finding volunteers for the church's educational ministry is nearly impossible. (Figure 8.1 B) This may have been communicated to me by others in the congregation, by my own previous experience or by both. (Figure 8.1 C & Figure 8.1 D)

I therefore anticipate no one will accept the position. (Figure 8.1 E) I never really ask if this anticipated result is accurate. I simply presume it is. My emotional response to this anticipated situation might be anxiety or fear. The superintendent's work will be dumped on my desk and I already have too much to do. Or I am uncomfortable asking for volunteers. They might say "No" and I always take this response as a personal rejection. So I become very anxious just thinking about finding a new superintendent (Figure 8.1 F)

I cannot think of many exceptions to this general mental map, so I go directly to making a decision based on my unexamined emotions and expectations.

Figure 8.1 Mental Mapping

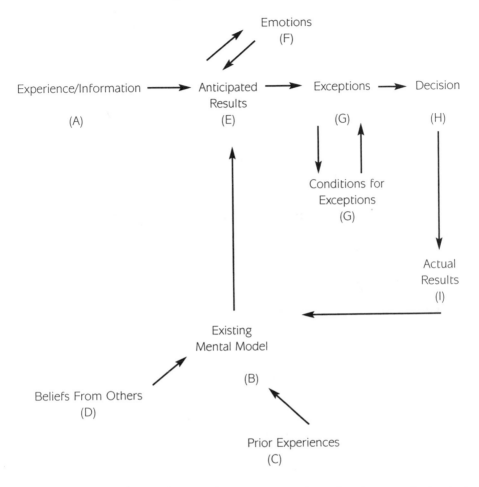

(Figure 8.1 H) I decide to pressure the current superintendent into continuing just another year. I use guilt-inducing strategies. I make promises I cannot keep. As a result, the superintendent reluctantly agrees to continue for a little while longer. (Figure 8.1 I)

Unfortunately, his efforts are minimal because he really did not want to be superintendent. A great deal of the work ends up on my desk anyway. I feel frustrated with him and also fearful he might quit if I say anything critical. As a result, I am paralyzed. The educational ministries flounder. Everyone loses. My unexamined mental model results in my taking actions that do not get the results I really want.

But what if my mental model is not correct? What if it really is possible to find someone else to be superintendent? I have acted on an assumption that may or may not be based in reality. I have allowed anticipated results and my emotional responses to them to push me into a decision that actually undermines my own long-term interest in a strong Christian education ministry. Mapping people's emotional responses to anticipated outcomes and how these emotions color their decisions is a crucial task. Often the distortions in people's perceptions and decisions occur at precisely this point.

People discover new freedom and unexpected possibilities if they can break the automatic links between events, anticipated outcomes, and emotional responses to these outcomes. Too often people have an experience, make an interpretation of what it means, respond to this interpretation based on old emotional patterns, and quickly reach a decision that lessens their anxiety, fear, embarrassment, or frustration. Once people break this automatic processing of experience, they can examine the distortions, deletions, overgeneralizations, or errors in their mental maps.

Coaches slow down people's acting so they can examine their underlying thinking. As people critically reflect on their unspoken mental models, they can take more intentional and powerful actions, which really do move them toward the results they want. Working with a coach, I might map out this situation and examine its assumptions.

- What if I changed my perspective that volunteers are impossible to find?
- What if I instead adopted a perspective that God had already provided the superintendent needed for this particular moment in the congregation's life?
- What other prior experiences might lead me to a different rule of thumb?
- What exceptions could exist to this general rule I have made up about volunteers?
- How do my emotional responses to anticipated results get in the way of making good decisions?
- Where do these emotional response come from and are they appropriate for the situation?
- What other decisions might I take that could lead to alternative outcomes?

When people take action, they are revealing their underlying assumptive perspectives. If coaches can slow down their thinking enough to tease out these unspoken mental maps, people can better understand the thinking that has produced the results they are getting. They can then brainstorm alternative "rules of thumb" or general beliefs that might produce different decisions, which could lead to the results clients are actually seeking in their lives.

Of course, a client's actual map will undoubtedly be much more complex than any of these simple scenarios. Regardless of the added complexity, encouraging clients to map their thinking allows them to re-claim their own power of choice. So long as these maps remain hidden from view, clients can feel they are victims of events over which they have no power.

COMMON ERRORS IN MENTAL MAPS

As clients map out their thinking, they realize the flaws and gaps in their own thinking. These flaws usually fall into several predictable categories. (Bandler & Grinder 1975) (Figure 8.2)

Figure 8.2 Common Errors in Mental Maps

COMMON ERRORS	CHARACTERISTICS	COACHING RESPONSE
Overgeneralization	Use words like: —everybody —nobody —always —never	Ask questions that encourage identification of exceptions
Vagueness	Use language that is vague, lacks specificity	Ask questions that encourage detail, specifics, examples
Distortions	Misinterprets how things are related.	Ask questions that encourage distance, objectivity, analysis that fills in gaps or sees relationships Ask questions that encourage client to see emotional responses are not cause or explanation of decision or behavior
Freeze Frames	Uses nouns rather than verbs to describe situations. Sees situations as static and unchangeable	Ask questions that encourage seeing the whole process rather than a single event. Facilitate awareness of how choices are possible.
Deletions	Ask what is being left out, ignored.	Ask client to make clear the links and steps in thinking. Use paraphrasing to fill into gaps.

One of the most obvious flaws is overgeneralization. People overgeneralize from a few experiences. We are in the land of overgeneralization when people use words such as

- Everybody
- Nobody
- Always
- Never
- Forever

When people overgeneralize, they miss the nuances and subtle cues that could guide them to alternative decisions. One way to break the power of overgeneralization is to encourage people to identify exceptions that qualify their rules of thumb. Coaches can ask questions such as "Who specifically does this?" or, "Under what conditions does this not happen?" As we saw in our example of the lights going out in the kitchen, the more exceptions that qualify one's general belief, the more choices people see and the greater power they experience.

Vagueness serves the same purpose as overgeneralization. Options and relationships are always fuzzy or blurry so long as they remain vague and ill-defined. Clarifying questions encourage clients to specify their maps so that relationships, links, and errors in thinking come into clearer focus. Once these difficulties in a client's mental model of events becomes visible, the client has more sense of choice, freedom, and empowerment. When a client says something like "People are too busy now to volunteer for these kinds of responsibilities," the coach needs to ask:

- What people?
- What specific responsibilities?
- What does being too busy look like?

Coaches can also ask catalytic questions that encourage people to explore distortions in their mental maps. When we distort, we misinterpret how things are related. They believe, for example that their emotions are caused by events or that their emotions cause events. Otis says, "Jerry makes me angry when he comes late to our Christian education committee meeting." The emotional response is seen as caused by the behavior. If we unpack our response, we might begin to see that Otis interprets Jerry's late arrival as a sign of disrespect for him as chairperson. But that is only an interpretation. There may be several other explanations for why Jerry comes late that have nothing to do with Otis. If coaches believe distortion is at work, they might explore with clients other possible combinations of cause-and-effect. The goal is to help the person see they have distorted a link or misidentified a link between two or more experiences.

Another common error involves confusing fixed conditions with fluid possibilities. When this occurs, people's maps describe everything using nouns rather than verbs. People consequently do not see processes. They only see nouns. They look only at the boxes in their mental maps, not the arrows. Yet the arrows are where their freedom to choose resides. A huge difference exists between saying "I am sorry that I made the decision to serve on the long-range planning committee" and "I am sorry that I am deciding to continue serving on the long-range planning committee." The first statement leaves no room for one's freedom to make another choice. The second permits the speaker to recognize his or her power to choose. Simply substituting the very *am deciding* for the noun *decision* creates a completely different perspective on the situation.

Substituting nouns for verbs is a lot like freeze frame photography. People can freeze one particular frame in a fluid, dynamic process. They then see only this one frame and not the whole process. They see a picture of the soccer player caught mid-air with the ball, but not the fluid motions running toward it nor the graceful follow-through afterwards.

Finally, our maps can delete important details. A client says to her coach, "I have to make better decisions." A lot has been left out of this statement. "Better than what?" one might wonder, or, "Decisions about what?" This person's deletions make it difficult to know what he or she means—let alone what to do next. Decisions are always about something. They always occur in certain contexts. Having listened skillfully to this client, a coach might ask questions such as

- Better decisions about what? Is it possible that you are already making good decisions about some things (such as deciding to seek help about making decisions) so you only need to work on another area of decision making?
- What does a good decision look like? What does a better decision look like?

Coaches can use paraphrasing when clients are deleting important parts of their maps. Paraphrasing does not mean just repeating back what someone has said. It can also mean filling in the deletions to help the client hear how you are completing their thoughts. Yujian says, "I have trouble communicating." So the coach does *not* say, "I hear you saying you have a difficult time communicating. Is that right?" A better response might be, "I hear you saying you hold back from saying things that might be viewed as critical or uncomplimentary to people who have some authority over you. Is that correct?"

People learn to take more powerful actions toward their goals when they can reflect on the cognitive and emotional forces that shaped previous actions. Effective coaching creates a courageous, safe space where people can slow down the forward action of their lives long enough to reflect and learn how to improve the accuracy, velocity, and clarity of their actions.

CHAPTER NINE

WHAT'S NEXT?

By now, you should realize that this chapter title is also a great coaching question! As you finish these chapters, you may be asking yourself: "What's next?"

Some of you may want to incorporate coaching skills into your existing ministries as Christian educators, heads of staff, or pastors. You really do not see yourself as a coach; but coaching skills could improve your practice of ministry. Others of you may be trying to discern if you are called to a part- or full-time ministry of coaching. Still others may be church planters who want to know more about coaching in order to work more effectively with your own coaches. Some readers may be members of regional church bodies. You are interesting in coaching because it could be yet another resource in your toolkit for nurturing and transforming congregations in your district, conference, presbytery, or region.

As you think about your next steps, you may want to explore whether you have some of the gifts and graces for coaching. Look back over the qualities of the coaching relationship and ask yourself whether you can claim these qualities for yourself. Which can you celebrate? Which require some nurture and attention?

Or you might want to assess whether you possess the specific skills associated with coaching. Looking back over these skills, which ones best characterize your strengths? Which ones represent areas where you might need to stretch and grow? Where could you gain skills or improve those you already have? A number of specialized training programs exist for preparing coaches. These are listed on the International Coach Federation website. One of the best ways to learn to coach is to have a coach. You might make a commitment to find a coach for yourself as a first step into coaching.

If you want to incorporate coaching skills into your existing ministries, which ones are most relevant? You may want to make a list of tools or strategies you can use now. Then develop a plan for incorporating them into your ministry. Make a commitment to take specific action within the next week or month. Then, at the end of this period, write another appointment with yourself into your calendar. Use this appointment to review your plan and see where you are.

You could also gather together a few persons you believe might be interested in coaching. Invite them to study this resource as a group. Group members could discuss a chapter, then practice coaching one another. One person would coach, another be coached, and a third would give feedback. After 30 minutes, the roles could rotate. The process would repeat itself until every person had coached, been coached, and observed. This pattern of study and practice would be a powerful tool for learning to coach.

Whatever you do next, remember that coaching is a ministry. As a coach, you share in Barnabas' ministry of encouragement—a ministry that multiplies leadership and equips the saints for the work of proclamation, witness, and service. Coaching is an opportunity to collaborate not just with another person but with the Holy Spirit in bringing out the best in another Christian's life and ministry. Even more importantly, it is an opportunity to see people through God's eyes: To see them in all their magnificence and beauty, courage and giftedness.

Coaches have the privilege of walking alongside others, catching a fleeting glimpse of their inner magnificence, and seeing them become who they already are in God's eyes. "Beloved, we are God's children now; what we will be has not yet been revealed. What we do know is this: when he is revealed, we will be like him, for we will see him as he is." (1 John 3:2)

GLOSSARY

Accountability. When a client identifies an action or agrees to coaching homework between sessions, the coach will ask for how the client plans to be accountable for these actions. The coach usually asks:

- What actions are you going to take?
- What is your timeline for these actions?; and
- How do you want to let me or others know when you have completed these actions?

Acknowledgement. Coaches acknowledge who someone is, not what they do. Acknowledgement recognizes someone's unique, inner attributes and values. Acknowledging clients' inner strengths validates these qualities when they may be having trouble seeing them for themselves. Acknowledgement includes both the delivery of the acknowledgement and checking for its reception by the client.

Asking for permission. If coaches wish to explore a sensitive area or an embarrassing topic, they ask permission before going there. Clients then have the responsibility for saying whether they want this discussion or not. The client can make one of three responses.

- Yes
- No
- Counter-offer ("Not now, but later," or, "Not about that topic but maybe this one.")

The coach must be prepared, if the client says "no," to respect the client's wishes.

Asking for the bottom line. Asking for the bottom line means asking for the essence or meaning behind the story rather than the whole story itself

Challenging. A challenge is like a request, only it goes beyond the client's comfort level. Most clients have self-imposed limits as to what they think is possible for them. A good challenge asks clients to take actions significantly beyond these self-imposed limits. A coach knows they have issued a challenge when the client gasps or exclaims, "I can't possibly do that!"

Championing. Coaches champion their clients when they remind them of their strengths, abilities, resourcefulness, and courage. They remind them they are capable human beings who can do much more than they imagine they can. Championing is somewhat like cheerleading or encouraging someone toward their goal when energy or commitment is flagging.

Confidentiality. Confidentiality means keeping information given by or about an individual secure from others. Confidentiality requires that coaches do not disclose that a particular person is or has been in a coaching relationship without that person's explicit, written permission. It also includes not sharing comments, stories, or observations that are made by the client during coaching. The obligation to maintain confidentiality does not typically end when the client dies. Confidentiality also applies to all forms of communication: verbal, written or electronic.

Feedback. Feedback involves telling people something they cannot discover on their own. If you ask me for feedback, I am giving you something you cannot get in any other way—my perception of your behavior.

Inquiry. An inquiry is a special kind of question that is not meant to be answered quickly but explored over time. Coaches typically pose a reflective inquiry at the end of a coaching session. The reflective inquiry is the client's homework assignment between appointments. Because clients live with a reflective inquiry between coaching sessions, it deepens their learning and action over time.

Intruding. When clients tell a story or begin to ramble into theories and generalizations, coaches intrude. They interrupt the client and ask him or her to state briefly the main point or to describe what action they plan to take. Intruding does not have to be rude or confrontational. But clients need to know that, in order to keep the coaching appointment brief and focused, the coach may intrude into a story or speculative rambling and ask the client to state succinctly the main idea.

Reframing. The process of changing one's perspective or assumptive framework is called re-framing. The purpose of re-framing is to help people experience their beliefs, actions, and values from different perspectives so they can have more flexibility and power of choice about what they do.

Requesting. Coaches may request that client's take particular actions, which they think may enhance learning or move the client further toward his or her goals. When a coach makes a request, the client can make one of three responses:

- "Yes"
- "No"
- "My counteroffer is…"

Resistance. Resistance is a natural and usually unconscious process of slowing or blocking progress toward significant change. It occurs when people realize that really changing their ministries means losing things that are comfortable, familiar, and precious. People resist because they become anxious about the unknown effects of their new actions. One positive aspect of resistance is that it allows people to consolidate past gains before moving forward again.

Structures. Structures are practical reminders that help people create focus and sustain commitment. Structures prompt clients into the actions to which they have committed themselves. Planners, calendars, to-do lists are all structures. So are taped reminders or even a string on one's finger.

References

Argyris, Chris. *Knowledge for Action: A Guide to Overcoming Barriers to Organizational Learning.* San Francisco: Jossey-Bass, 1993.

Bandler, Richard, and John Grinder. *The Structure of Magic I: A Book about Language and Therapy.* Palo Alto: Science and Behavior Books, 1975.

Bandy, Thomas. *Coaching Change: Breaking Down Resistance, Building Up Hope.* Nashville: Abingdon Press, 2000.

Barry, William A., and William J. Connolly. *The Practice of Spiritual Direction.* New York: Seabury Press, 1982.

Belf, Teri-E. *Coaching with Spirit: Allowing Success to Emerge.* San Francisco: Jossey-Bass/Pfeiffer, 2002.

Bromiley, Geoffrey W., ed. *Theological Dictionary of the New Testament: Abridged in One Volume.* Grand Rapids: William B. Eerdman's Publishing, 1985.

Covey, Stephen R. *The Seven Habits of Highly Effective People: Restoring the Character Ethic.* (New York: Fireside Book, 1990).

Crawford, Mike. "Coaching for Ministry Excellence." *Current 8,* no. 6 (October 17, 2003): 10.

Downey, Myles. *Effective Coaching: Lessons from the Coach's Coach.* New York: Texere, 2003.

Friedman, Edwin H., D.D. *A Failure of Nerve: Leadership in the Age of the Quick Fix.* Bethesda, MD: The Edwin Friedman Estate/Trust, 1999.

————. *Generation to Generation: Family Process in Church and Synagogue.* New York: The Guilford Press, 1985.

Grodzki, Lynn, ed. *The New Private Practice: Therapist-Coaches Share Stories, Strategies, and Advice.* New York: W. W. Norton & Company, 2002.

Hargrove, Robert. *Masterful Coaching: Inspire an "Impossible Future" While Producing Extraordinary Leaders and Extraordinary Results, Rev. ed.* San Francisco: Jossey-Bass/Pfeiffer, 2003.

Hendricks, William. *Coaching, Mentoring, and Managing.* Franklin Lakes, NJ: Career Press, 1996.

International Coach Federation. http://www.coachfederation.com

Kegan, Robert and Lisa Laskow Lahey. *How the Way We Talk Can Change the Way We Work: Seven Languages for Tranformation.* San Francisco: Jossey-Bass/Pfeiffer, 2001.

Killebrew, Katherine G. "The Role of the Presbytery of West Jersey in Congregational Redevelopment." D.Min. thesis, McCormick Theological Seminary, 2005.

Levinson, Daniel J. *The Seasons of a Man's Life.* New York: Ballantine Books, 1978.

Logan, Robert. http://coachnet.org.

Mace, Myles L. *The Growth and Development of Executives.* Boston: Harvard University Press, 1950.

Meinke, Lynn F. "Top Ten Indicators to Refer to a Mental Health Professional." http://www.coachfederation.org/regulatory/topten.asp.

Quinn, Robert E. *Deep Change: Discovering the Leader Within.* San Francisco: Jossey-Bass, 1996.

Russell, Letty M. *The Future of Partnership.* Philadelphia: Westminster Press, 1979.

Simpson, J and E. Weiner, eds. *The Oxford English Dictionary, 2nd Ed.* Oxford: Clarendon Press, 1987.

Roxburgh, Alan. *Crossing the Bridge: Church Leadership in a Time of Change.* The Percept Group, 2000.

Sellon, Mary K., Daniel P. Smith, and Gail F. Grossman. *Redeveloping the Congregation: A How-To for Lasting Change.* Bethesda: Alban Institute, 2003.

Senge, Peter M., Charlotte Roberts, Richard B. Ross; Bryan J. Smith, and Art Kleiner. *The Fifth Discipline Fieldbook: Strategies and Tools for Building a Learning Organization.* New York: Doubleday, 1994.

Toulmin, Stephen Edelston. *The Uses of Argument.* Cambridge: The University Press, 1958.

Whitworth, Laura, Henry Kimsey-House, and Phil Sandahl. *Co-Active Coaching: New Skills for Coaching People Toward Success in Work and Life.* Palo Alto, CA: Davis-Black Publishing, 1998.

Williams, Patrick and Deborah Davis. *Therapist as Life Coach: Transforming Your Practice.* New York: W. W. Norton & Company, 2002.